WHO DO YOU SAY THAT I AM?

Who Do You Say That I Am?

Exploring the Question of Christ

RICHARD GRIBBLE, CSC

Paulist Press
New York / Mahwah, NJ

Cover image by Inked Pixels / Shutterstock.com
Cover design by Joe Gallagher
Book design by Lynn Else

Library of Congress Cataloging-in-Publication Data
Names: Gribble, Richard, author.
Title: Who do you say that I am? : exploring the question of Christ / Richard Gribble, C.S.C., Ph.D.
Description: New York : Paulist Press, 2020. | Includes bibliographical references. | Summary: "Richard Gribble answers a central question of Jesus'ministry, looking at how Jesus and his various roles have been understood by Christians through the centuries. This book is an attempt to have the reader answer for herself or himself, "Who is Jesus for you?," and further one's relationship with Jesus. At the same time, it is also meant to be used for groups, as discussion questions are offered herein"— Provided by publisher.
Identifiers: LCCN 2019040792 (print) | LCCN 2019040793 (ebook) | ISBN 9780809155071 (paperback) | ISBN 9781587689062 (ebook)
Subjects: LCSH: Jesus Christ—Person and offices.
Classification: LCC BT203 .G747 2020 (print) | LCC BT203 (ebook) | DDC 232.8—dc23
LC record available at https://lccn.loc.gov/2019040792
LC ebook record available at https://lccn.loc.gov/2019040793

ISBN 978-0-8091-5507-1 (paperback)
ISBN 978-1-58768-906-2 (e-book)

Published by Paulist Press
997 Macarthur Boulevard
Mahwah, New Jersey 07430
www.paulistpress.com

Printed and bound in the
United States of America

At the outset of the rite of baptism, the priest or deacon says to the parents of the child, "In doing so [asking for baptism] you are accepting the responsibility of training her/him in the practice of the faith. It will be your duty to bring her/him up to keep God's commandments as Christ taught us by loving God and our neighbor." This extremely challenging statement, that parents are responsible for the faith development of their children, was certainly carried out in my life by my father and mother, Richard and Dorothy Gribble, and many wonderful friends. While my parents have long since passed to God, nevertheless for me the answers to the question of this book, "Who do you say that I am?" were initiated by them in word and action. Those same answers have been fostered by special friends who have helped me along the way. Thus, it is appropriate that this book be dedicated in memory to my parents and two special friends, Sister Tania and Christina, who have taught me many lessons and brought much joy to my life.

CONTENTS

INTRODUCTION

Scripture scholars tell us that the climax of St. Matthew's Gospel comes in chapter 16. We read,

> Now when Jesus came into the district of Caesarea Philippi, he asked his disciples, "Who do people say that the Son of Man is?" And they said, "Some say John the Baptist, but others Elijah, and still others Jeremiah or one of the prophets." He said to them, "But who do you say that I am?" Simon Peter answered, "You are the Messiah, the Son of the living God." (16:13–16)

Jesus's question to his disciples, "Who do you say that I am?" continues to challenge Christians today, for it prompts us to reexamine our basic relationship with the Lord. How we answer says something very fundamental and important about who we are and how we understand our connection with Jesus, and by extension the community of faith, the people of God, the Church, that he founded. Exploring this basic yet highly challenging question for Christians today is the purpose of this book.

CONTEMPORARY VIEWS OF JESUS

Based on two thousand years of Christian history and theology as well as one's personal religious training and education, contemporary Christians might answer Jesus's question as did Peter, that Christ is Messiah and Son of God, but there are many additional ways that the Lord may be understood. Reviewing these multiple understandings of Jesus can provide us with a broader context for and a deeper understanding of St. Peter's profound and insightful response. In order to understand the nature and development of various contemporary understandings of Jesus, it is first essential that the reader have a solid historical and theological foundation concerning what the Church teaches about Jesus and how this understanding was eventually defined. Today, the idea that Jesus is both human and divine rolls off our lips with nary a thought or a question. Few are aware, however, that the definition of Jesus being one person with two natures, namely human and divine, took over four centuries from the time of Christ to actually be defined. Only at the fourth worldwide (ecumenical) council of bishops, held at Chalcedon (present-day Turkey) in AD 451, were the words of the accepted definition actually produced. Few people are aware of the "war of words" that was waged between theologians, the various heresies that arose during this contentious time, and the condemnations that were proclaimed by Church officials against those who proclaimed ideas that in some minds seemed logical, but have been labeled as heresies historically.

With a firm foundation on the historical and theological understanding of Jesus, our exploration of the answer to the Lord's question to Peter can proceed forward. First, as would be true with the investigation of any religious question, we need to consult the basic source of our faith—the Bible. Thus, we need to look at the "Jesus of Scripture." What do the four Gospel evangelists primarily, and the various letters of St. Paul and the other New Testament writers, tell us about Jesus? When we read the Scriptures, what images and understandings of Christ attract us? In answering the basic question of our inquiry, what does the Bible say? Certainly, Scripture is understood differently by various people, yet there are some basic themes that run throughout the New Testament. Christ as teacher, miracle worker, and Redeemer, are only three of several examples that emerge from the pages of the New Testament. How can this most basic yet most significant part of Roman Catholicism's one source of revelation[1] help us to respond to our basic question?

One of Jesus's most repetitious patterns in the New Testament is his teaching on prayer, manifested both in his actions and words. One could easily understand Christ as the ultimate "pray-er," that is, one who actually prays. An examination of the Scriptures clearly shows that Jesus carried out the challenge that St. Paul would articulate a generation later in his Letter to the Ephesians (6:18) when he wrote, "Pray in the Spirit at all times in every prayer and supplication." Jesus prayed before all major decisions, spent whole nights in prayer, and prayed for those who were his friends and those who would remain when he left the world. Additionally, Jesus taught us how to pray. When answering how we understand Jesus, his life of prayer is certainly central.

After exploring how the New Testament helps us to answer Jesus's question, "Who do you say that I am?" we can review two seemingly opposed paradigms or models of one's understanding of Christ. The "earlier paradigm," so named because it was the first chronologically and still remains the most traditional view of the Lord, speaks of the "Jesus of Faith." For centuries, based largely on the information derived from Scripture and the aforementioned historical development, Christians have viewed Jesus as the divine human who came to the world at the command of the Father to atone for human sin and bring the possibility of redemption to all men and women. This answer to Jesus's basic question suggests that all the Bible narrates about Christ must be viewed through the eyes of faith. While certain events may be inexplicable and details either sketchy or inconsistent in various accounts presented by the evangelists, the reality of faith dominates one's perspective of Christ and, therefore, one's answer to the basic question. The "emerging paradigm," associated with the "Christ of History," emerged historically with the Enlightenment of the eighteenth century. This view of Jesus seeks more verifiable evidence in answering the basic question of who Jesus is for any particular person. While these two views of Jesus seem to have no compatibility, a contemporary Christian could easily hold both perspectives simultaneously, with, as might seem obvious, a preference for one paradigm over the other.

Whether we see Jesus more in faith or through history, it is clear from reading the Gospels that Jesus was someone who turned everything upside down. What seemed to be the norm for Jewish society was challenged by Jesus in many ways. In essence, he turned what was normal on its head; he was a reverser of roles. How could it be true that "the last will be first, and the first will be last" (Matt 20:16), "all who exalt themselves will be humbled, and those who humble themselves will be exalted" (Luke 14:11), and "the sabbath was made for humankind, and not humankind for the sabbath" (Mark 2:27). Jesus was one who sought to transform Jewish thought, substituting compassion for the law, treating Gentiles with courtesy and love, and accepting those who were unacceptable to society.

Jesus's ministry as a reverser of roles led directly to his death. Why was Jesus executed? For many the basic answer to the question of Matthew 16:15 is that Jesus is the Redeemer, that he was sent into the world specifically to die in atonement for all human failures, those that occurred before, during, and after his physical life on earth. Yet, why was Jesus executed? What did he do that was so onerous that it led to capital punishment? While times were different, and Roman law is different than our own, even a cursory examination of the Scriptures tells us that Jesus did nothing that was punishable by death. Thus, the question remains: Why *was* Jesus executed? The basic answer is that his behavior, as far as Jewish leaders were concerned, was so threatening to their societal norms that the religious elite sought his death.

While Jesus was turning everything on its head and challenging preconceived notions of what was right and wrong, he was simultaneously proclaiming the kingdom of God. Many of Christ's parables in the Synoptic Gospels (Matthew, Mark, and Luke) are proclaimed as similes for the kingdom of God. Yet, it is not obvious what the Lord means. Was the kingdom of God a political system that he sought to inaugurate? Was it a present reality that he sought to construct and nurture during his public ministry? Is it a future "place" where our eternal life with God will be lived? Exploring these various understandings of the kingdom of God can help us to better answer our question under investigation.

Various understandings of the kingdom of God can largely be attributed to how we view and respond to contemporary culture. Today's world, as we know, is becoming increasingly more secularized, with, it seems unfortunately, more and more people believing that they have no need for organized religion. To be a Christian today and remain loyal to the basic precepts articulated by Jesus in the Gospels almost necessitates that we be countercultural, that we challenge many of the prevailing "truths" that contemporary life and its prophets have proclaimed as valid today. For many, the eternal truths of Christ and two thousand years of Christian thought have taken flight and are no longer applicable. Thus, in answering our basic question, we must ask where Jesus fits in with our contemporary culture. What place do he and his teachings have as we stand approximately one-fifth of the way through the twenty-first century?

Placing Jesus within the contemporary context of twenty-first-century life forces us to ask ourselves how we interpret the teaching of Jesus today. In seeking to answer the basic question of Matthew 16:15, contemporary Christians must ask some serious and extremely challenging questions. Are the teachings of Jesus relevant for today's world? Can we apply Jesus's teachings and understanding of life today as in the past? In other words, are the teachings of Jesus timeless or more time-dependent? Have we allowed contemporary society to sway us from the absolute truths of Christ's teaching that have guided men and women of faith for some two thousand years? When answering Jesus's question, contemporary Christians will be forced to interpret Jesus's teaching and how it applies to people in today's world.

Armed with a modern interpretation as to how Jesus's mission and teaching can be helpful today, we close our examination of Jesus's challenging question by asking how his words help us when we make moral decisions. We make decisions every day; most of them are small, routine, and rather insignificant. However, at times more fundamental and difficult decisions must be made, many of which have various moral dimensions. There is a need, therefore, to explore how we might apply the teachings of Jesus to moral decisions today. This again, as stated above, requires us to ask how applicable the message of Jesus, articulated in both word and deed some two thousand years ago, has relevance today.

HOW TO USE THIS BOOK

Since prayer and spirituality are central tenets to the Christian life, this book seeks to further one's relationship with the Lord Jesus through the basic exploration of the central question of Jesus, as articulated in St. Matthew's Gospel: "Who do you say that I am?" Readers can certainly benefit from an exploration of this central question, utilizing the chapters and discussion questions that follow as a means of rediscovering Jesus in a personal way. The chapters are intentionally short, not overly laden with in-depth and complicated theological ideas, and are written in a straightforward manner that, it is hoped, can be useful as well as challenging to all Christians.

While individual use of this volume can be very helpful in broadening one's perspective and deepening one's faith, this book can also be utilized by groups. All have experienced how one person's ideas lead others to think more broadly. We have all been in discussions during which one person makes a comment about an idea that prior to that moment we had never considered. Thus, thoughts and reflections by others can help us to see ideas and be introduced to opinions that we probably would never have considered. Thus, this volume can be effectively used as a tool for faith-sharing groups, parish adult education classes, and diocesan renewal programs as three common applications. The discussion questions are poised to both challenge readers and enliven discussion. I claim neither extraordinary insight nor absolute command of any of the views of Jesus presented in the various chapters of this book. Thus, readers would be wise to challenge the ideas presented in the text and bring their own thoughts to their reading and group discussions.

Since there is no absolutely correct answer to Jesus's question to his apostles, the variety of answers that readers may raise when utilizing this volume is indeed instructive. There is no one absolute way to understand Jesus of Nazareth. How one understands the Word of God, the second person of the Blessed Trinity, who became incarnate through the power of the Holy Spirit in the womb of the Blessed Virgin Mary, is very personal. It is hoped, however, that taking the journey that this book describes, whether that be as an individual or in a group setting, can be an instructive and growth-filled experience. Hopefully the reader will discover more things about Jesus, but also and equally if not more importantly, grow in one's self-knowledge, and thus better understand where one stands in his or her relationship with our Lord. It is my hope and prayer that your exploration of Jesus's great question, "Who do you say that I am?" will advance your love of God and neighbor, make you better prepared for the faith challenges in this life, and move you one step closer to eternal life, God's promise to all who believe.

Chapter 1

WHO IS JESUS?

Contemporary Christians, like their predecessors of the past two thousand years, remain fascinated with Jesus and seek to know more about him. This fascination with the person, message, mission, and life of Christ is visible through the filmmaking industry. "The Robe," produced in 1953; "King of Kings," which hit the theaters in 1961; and the popular miniseries "Jesus of Nazareth," which played on television in 1977, show Jesus's popularity through time. They are still viewed by many, especially during the Christmas and Easter seasons. Mel Gibson's 2004 production, "The Passion of the Christ," while controversial in the minds of some, so powerfully depicted events of the paschal mystery, the passion, death, and resurrection of Jesus, that audiences were stunned into silence and didn't move from their seats as the credits rolled at the end of the film. More recently still, the film "Risen" (2016) depicted the life of one of the Roman centurions present on Calvary, and how the resurrection transformed him into a follower of Christ. Fascination with what could have been events in the early life of Jesus are depicted in another 2016 film, "The Young Messiah." Quite obviously, the subject of "Who is Jesus?" is indeed a topic of great interest that has captivated Christians for centuries and continues to fascinate them today.

CONTEMPORARY VIEWS AND IMAGES OF JESUS

Hollywood's fascination with Jesus, and the varied ways in which he is depicted on film, is reinforced by contemporary images of the Lord, some of which have long and deep roots in the Christian tradition. Certainly, the most basic and traditional view of Christ is to see his role as the Redeemer. From the time of the original sin of Adam and Eve, God developed a plan, which theologians call "Salvation History," to save humanity and provide a path to life eternal with God. The Lord's plan was inaugurated by the call of Abraham. The Book of Genesis (12:1–2) reads,

> Now the LORD said to Abram, "Go from your country and your kindred and your father's house to the land that I will show you. I will make of you a great nation, and I will bless you, and make your name great, so that you will be a blessing."

God's plan for humanity, initiated through the covenant between the Hebrews and himself, continued with the formation of the nation of Israel and their series of kings, the division of the nation into Israel and Judah, and eventually the loss of the Northern Kingdom (Israel) in 722 BCE. Despite Judah's (Southern Kingdom) lack of fidelity, the nation continued, enduring the infamous Babylonian Exile and return (587–537 BCE), and leading eventually to the birth of Jesus and his sacrificial death. The other traditional view of Jesus is his that he is a divine human, two natures in one person, ultimately defined at the fourth ecumenical council at Chalcedon (in modern Turkey) in 451 CE.

More contemporary views of Christ are largely based on a basic difference in how one understands Jesus. Some people view Jesus as far beyond human understanding; as God, he is seen as almost unapproachable, far beyond human reach. This image of Jesus views him as a judge, one who will return at the end of time and punish us unless we stay on the straight and narrow path. Those who understand Jesus in this way (known theologically as "high" Christology) are ready for the Lord's return, the second coming, realizing, as the Scriptures say, we do not know the day or the hour (Matt 24:36). Some people view Jesus as imminently close to us at all times. He is the one who celebrates with us in all our triumphs and walks closely with us and dries our tears during moments of defeat and sadness. This is the Jesus of the famous "Footprints" poem, who reminds us, "During your times of trial and suffering, when you see only one set of footprints, it was then that I carried you." Roles that arise from this image of Jesus (known theologically as "low" Christology) would be teacher, miracle worker, advocate for the poor, man of compassion, as well as the stern challenger of authority. The various views that contemporary Christians hold of Jesus are thus related to the basic question under investigation, "Who is Jesus for me?"

TWO CONTRASTING PARADIGMS

Contemporary studies of Jesus have developed two different images, largely historically based, which are viewed by many to be opposed, but are understood by others to be compatible. The Protestant biblical scholar Marcus Borg, in his book *Meeting Jesus Again for the First Time*, outlines the characteristics of what he calls the earlier and emerging paradigms.[1]

Historically the first and certainly the most common understanding of Jesus, the earlier model, is belief centered; it is rooted in a faith conception of Christ. This model emphasizes a more literal understanding of Christian language. It comprises four essential characteristics. First, Jesus is seen through his role as a teacher of doctrine. Those who hold this model gladly profess precise teachings with respect to Jesus. Second, the Gospels and Jesus are seen as historically certain. This need not mean that what the Bible precisely says is exactly what happened, but rather that there are no serious errors. As *Dei Verbum*, Vatican II's Dogmatic Constitution on Divine Revelation, states concerning the four Gospels,

> The sacred authors wrote the four Gospels, selecting some things from the many which had been handed on by word of mouth or in writing, reducing some of them to a synthesis, explaining some things in view of the situation of their churches and preserving the form of proclamation but always in such fashion that they told us the honest truth about Jesus. (para. 19)[2]

Third, Christians who are attracted to the earlier paradigm centered themselves in belief and faith. For them, Jesus is closely linked to the afterlife. One believes in Jesus today for the sake of heaven tomorrow. Jesus's message and redemptive death are all about the attainment of heaven for believers. Finally, prior to the Enlightenment, this belief-centered model referred to faith in Jesus. In the post-Enlightenment world, the idea behind faith shifted. Christians began to say that belief in some truth, such as the life and mission of Jesus, required that the authority and tradition of the past be replaced by experimentation and verification.

While the earlier paradigm, both historically and certainly numerically, with its faith-centered core, has dominated Christian thinking, the post-Enlightenment world, as described by Borg, offers a more historical and scientific view of Christ. Rather than viewing the Gospels and other New Testament books as products of faith, advocates for this emerging paradigm suggest that the Gospels are historical products, a combination of past memory and metaphorical stories. In this view, the Gospels are not seen as God's story of Jesus, but rather Christianity's story of Jesus. Thus, the Gospels are viewed as a product of a historical process; they are documents that present how the first Christians sought to bring the message and mission of Christ to the polytheistic and Jewish world, beginning in the Eastern Mediterranean region and moving over the centuries to every corner of the world.

There is, thus, a crucial distinction between the earlier and the emerging paradigms. The former, centered in belief, can envision Jesus only through the eyes of faith. Everything that Jesus said or did is understood through the filter that Christ is indeed the resurrected Savior of the world. Thus, Jesus is seen as a post-Easter figure. Such a view allows one to readily accept stories of the Gospel without hesitation. The emerging paradigm, on the other hand, seeks to place Jesus within the historical context of first-century Palestine. Christ is seen as a historical figure who walked the earth, taught important lessons, and performed many good deeds. While the basic message of the Gospels is clear, the precise historical accuracy of these texts is questioned.

TITLES FOR JESUS

These two contrasting paradigms are illustrated in the Scriptures through the various titles that are ascribed to the Lord. In his initial question, Jesus asked the disciples, "Who do people say that the Son of Man is?" The responses that he receives, John the Baptist, Elijah, Jeremiah, or another prophet, illustrate the pre-Easter, emerging paradigm that emphasizes the historical Jesus. All of the names suggested are historical people, well known by the Jews of Jesus's day; there is no indication that Jesus is anything more than a man of history. While probably viewing Jesus as an important individual, who possessed great abilities as a teacher and was probably close to God from his ability to perform miraculous cures, the answers of "the people" provide no evidence that Jesus is divine. Of course, to claim that Christ was a divine figure would have been considered by the Jews as heretical, violating the basic principle of monotheism. The response of the people is understandable, for the aforementioned reason, as well as the fact that Jesus's question was posed before the resurrection.

It is interesting, therefore, that without verifiable evidence and holding an unacceptable belief, still Peter responded to Jesus's question in such a different way. Not only does he call him the Messiah, but also the Son of God. Peter could rightly have understood Jesus to be the Messiah, for indeed the long-awaited Messiah was to be both a human and a kingly figure who would be a great champion for the Hebrews.[3] However, Peter's response goes much deeper, claiming that Jesus is divine. The Lord tells him that his insight has come from God:

> Blessed are you, Simon son of Jonah! For flesh and blood has not revealed this to you, but my Father in heaven. (Matt 16:17)

It did not take long for the post-Easter paradigm, Borg's earlier model centered on faith, to dominate the titles ascribed to Jesus. Almost immediately the Christian community added Christ to Jesus's title, indicative that he was indeed the long-awaited Messiah. More importantly, however, the name of Jesus Christ was integrally linked with "Lord" and "Son of God." It should be noted that the term "Son of God" was a title widely used by Near

Eastern religions. Additionally, some in Israel saw the nation as God's firstborn son. The use of the term "Son of God" by Peter is seen by Scripture scholars more as evidence of the apostle's faith. Thus, Peter makes a direct link between Jesus and God. The earlier paradigm, seeing him through the lens of faith and creeds, was established and would remain basically unchallenged until the eighteenth century and the dawn of the Enlightenment.

When looking at the titles for Jesus, the names given him by others are only half of the equation; what did Jesus call himself? The term "Son of Man" is used exclusively by Jesus in the New Testament save one reference (in Acts 7:56). While Jesus repeatedly uses the title "Son of Man" for himself, as reported by the Synoptic evangelists, in John's Gospel exclusively, Jesus refers to himself in seven "I am" statements. Dispersed throughout the Fourth Gospel, Jesus says, "I am the bread of life" (6:48), "...the light of the world" (8:12), "...the gate" (10:9), "...the good shepherd" (10:14), "...the way, and the truth, and the life" (14:6), "...the vine" (15:5), and "...the resurrection and the life" (11:25). These titles are highly significant as the knowledgeable Jew of Jesus's time would have made a direct link between Jesus's words and God. The Book of Exodus describes Moses's encounter with God. Moses views a bush that is burning but not consumed by the fire. Realizing that he is conversing with Yahweh, Moses asks God,

> "If I come to the Israelites and say to them, 'The God of your ancestors has sent me to you,' and they ask me, 'What is his name?' what shall I say to them?" God said to Moses, "I AM WHO I AM."' He said further, "Thus you shall say to the Israelites, 'I AM has sent me to you.'" (Exod 3:13–14)

Thus, Jesus is claiming again and again that he is associated with the Hebrew God, making himself divine. Clearly, the author of John's Gospel wants his readers to understand that Jesus is God.

JESUS AND AMERICAN CHRISTIANITY TODAY

Today in the United States, Christianity, including the Roman Catholic community, is divided in its understanding of Jesus. While it is clear that this division exists denominationally with a plethora of varied Christian groups, the split between those who hold the "emerging paradigm" compared with those who hold to the "earlier paradigm" is also significant. One is not clearly more true, accurate, or relevant. But it does set up a contrast between those who are more conservative (recall the "earlier paradigm" model) with those who are more progressive (the "emerging paradigm" model).

Those who hold greater value in the earlier paradigm are generally more community centered, finding strength through the common denominator of traditional faith. The advance of history, archaeology, and other disciplines that might shed additional light on the message and meaning of the Scriptures, while appreciated, are not of any great significance in how one views Jesus. These Christians are content to view Christ as the resurrected Savior; they understand the Scriptures from this perspective.

This earlier paradigm's perspective, while clear and evident in the lives of many active Christians, is also present in another public manifestation, the "Christian Right." Some more conservative and traditional individuals and groups, seeking to hold back the tide of growing secularism, have banded together to stand for values, particularly moral issues, that are found in contemporary public debate. These people hold strongly to the pro-life agenda, support traditional marriage, and adhere to the conventional story of Creation as presented in the Book of Genesis. While they are in the majority numerically, some today hold these views as anti-intellectual and (at least in the minds of some) bigoted. Yet, the earlier model holds eternal truths that cannot be measured by time or intellectual and scientific advancement.

Promoters of the emerging paradigm take a more progressive perspective in their general approach to Christian thought. Rather than utilizing the traditional geographical parish, members of this group often seek communities of intention and commitment, groups where similar views on contemporary issues bind individuals into a community. Commitment to adult theological education and employing the principles of social justice as a base upon which Christianity must flourish are strong principles in this more contemporary view of Christ. As with the critique of the earlier paradigm, however, some suggest that the emerging paradigm, if not curbed or brought under some umbrella, can lead to religious indifferentism. If one's view of Jesus is not centered in a faith dimension, then any particular Christian perspective that fits the need of the individual would be acceptable.

While it seems that these paradigms stand in opposition, there is indeed value in both, and therefore there is every possibility that one can stand simultaneously in both camps. In answering our basic question, "Who is Jesus?" we see that both paradigms answer the question. One's image of the Lord is obviously directly related to and even predicts the answer to the question. Other important questions that come from Scripture or Christian tradition can also be answered through either model. For example, we often hear, "Jesus loves me, this I know, for the Bible tells me so." What does this statement imply if one holds the more traditional earlier paradigm as opposed to a more contemporary emerging view of Jesus? A person holding the earlier paradigm might suggest that Jesus's death on the cross demonstrated his great love. One drawn to the emerging model might view Jesus's radical emphasis on compassion (to be addressed in detail in a later chapter) instead of adherence to the staid Mosaic Law as more central. The powerful message of John 3:16, "For God so loved the world that he gave his only Son, so that everyone who believes in him may not perish but may have eternal life," will also generate various meanings depending on how a person addresses the earlier versus emerging paradigm question. Does Jesus exist for the sake of the world, or is Christ, in the words of St. John, suggesting something else about his mission?

Answering the above questions and similar ones will lead many to find themselves either moving between camps, or more likely finding comfort in both. Pope Emeritus Benedict XVI, in his Christological trilogy, *Jesus of Nazareth*, asked a pointed question: "Where is the post-Easter faith supposed to have come from if Jesus laid no foundation for it before Easter?"[4] Clearly the pope suggests that the pre- and post-Easter images of Jesus are linked, with the former dependent upon the latter. Thus, the idea that one can have feet in both camps is clearly established and recognized.

CONCLUSION

How contemporary people view Jesus shapes the Christian life they live. Hence, toward the outset of this investigation, it is essential for readers to challenge themselves by asking where they fall in the spectrum of the earlier and the emerging paradigms. Most, I suspect, will find themselves primarily in one camp or the other, but others will find great comfort with feet in both communities. Why cannot one have strong faith in Christ as a resurrected Lord, while at the same time suggest that the Scriptures provide evidence to the reality of the historical Jesus and his message of hope for the world? Clearly Christian identity and loyalty are shaped in many ways by denomination, but they are also shaped by one's image of Jesus. Who is Jesus for you? Asking the question is the first step; taking the time to contemplate an answer is our responsibility as well.

Discussion Questions

1. Which title(s) for Jesus is/are most attractive to you and why?
2. Do you find a strong attraction to either the earlier or emerging paradigms? What factors associated with these concepts are attractive?
3. Which of the seven "I am" statements in John's Gospel is most attractive to you and why?
4. In your opinion, is it a contradiction in terms to state that one can have feet in both camps, both the earlier and emerging paradigms, simultaneously?
5. Do you experience, either within yourself or within your community of faith, a division created by various images of Jesus? If this is your experience, is such diversity helpful or hurtful to both the local and universal Church?

Chapter 2

WHAT THE CHURCH TEACHES ABOUT JESUS

If one asked a Christian with the age and maturity of a teenager or older the question, "What does the Church teach about Jesus Christ?" the basic answer would be straightforward and simple: Jesus is the Son of God, both human and divine. This answer would roll off the tongue of most faithful Christians. Yet this seemingly simple and straightforward answer was not obvious to our ancestors in the faith, especially those who lived in the first centuries after Jesus. As we will see, it took over four centuries for the Church to clearly define that Jesus was not only the Son of God, but in some inexplicable way fully human at the same time. This basic teaching of the Church developed over time as men and women of faith struggled to understand and clearly define Jesus and his relationship to the Father and the Holy Spirit. In the process, several ideas that have since been declared heresies arose, necessitating Church action to stamp out these errant beliefs and guide the bark of Peter back into safe and calm waters. The story of how the teaching of the Church concerning Jesus was developed must be an initial building block in our investigation of the basic question of this book: "Who do you say that I am?"

THE NEED TO DEFINE JESUS

The minority status of Christianity in the land of its origins, Israel, prompted those first followers of Jesus to better understand Christ and his relationship to God. After Jesus's ascension to his Father in heaven, the Acts of the Apostles, referred to by some as "The Fifth Gospel," tells us that the apostles and other disciples of Jesus found themselves as a persecuted group. The Jewish religious leaders who had taken such great offense to Jesus, due to his countercultural approach to Judaism—proclaiming compassion to be greater than the law, violating many precepts of the Sabbath, and challenging the religious elite on their hypocrisy—were equally diligent in their persecution of the Lord's followers. Despite the odds against them, the fledgling Christian community persevered.

Two other great events, one specific and one more general, added urgency to the need for Christians to better understand Jesus. Following the Jewish revolt against the Roman occupation of Israel in the year 66 CE, the Romans destroyed the Jewish temple and most of Jerusalem prompting the great Jewish Diaspora in the year 70 CE. The Jews and the initial converts to Christianity, all of whom like Jesus and the apostles were Jewish, left their ancestral home, scattered throughout Europe, and settled wherever they could find peace. The more general situation that prompted Christians to define Jesus was the Roman persecutions. Beginning as early as the mid-first century through the action of the infamous Emperor Nero (54–69 CE) and continuing on both local and empire-wide levels, Romans persecuted Christians, leading many to become martyrs. The Romans accused Christians of being politically indifferent, of refusing military service, of performing magic (a reference to the celebration of the Eucharist), and of holding, from the Roman perspective, unacceptable views toward chastity and marriage. On top of all this, of course, Christians, like Jews, were monotheistic and refused to pay homage to the Roman pantheon of gods. This situation continued until the Emperor Constantine issued the "Edict of Toleration" in 311 CE, mandating freedom of religion for all in the empire.

The minority status of Christians, and their struggle to maintain their beliefs in the face of severe persecution, prompted Church members to better define and even in some ways systematize their understanding of Jesus. Thus the Church developed a creed, or a series of beliefs, that helped Christians to better understand their faith and stand against the tide of opposition they experienced. Christians sought to define how they experienced Jesus and to clarify their complex understanding of God, which we call the Trinity. Additionally, there was a need to correct misunderstandings that may have arisen in this general effort to understand the Lord, as well as to distinguish Christians from other religious sects that were present in the Eastern Mediterranean world during the first few centuries after Christ. Thus, we see in the writings of several prominent early Christians the first attempts to better define Christ and his relationship to God. One second-century document by St. Justin Martyr (his *First Apology*) describes the regional baptism formula, articulated originally in Matthew 28, acknowledging God to be Father, Son, and Holy Spirit. In the third century another famous theologian, Tertullian, wrote his "Rule of Faith," which positively contributed to the definition that early Christians held about Jesus. Ultimately, in the late third century, Hippolytus wrote "the Apostles' Creed," which clearly speaks of Jesus and his relationship with the Father and the Holy Spirit.

THE DEVELOPMENT OF THE CHURCH'S TEACHING

However, although "the Apostles' Creed," was a giant leap forward, competing interests and the ideas of certain individuals prompted the Church to do more and in an official way define how it understood Jesus. In the early fourth century in Alexandria, Egypt, a priest named Arius claimed that Jesus was not God, but rather a "superhuman" intercessor between humanity and God. His rationale for this understanding was based on passages he had read in the Bible. In Psalm 2:7 and Hebrews 5:5, he read, "You are my Son; today I have begotten you." Arius suggested that if the Son was begotten, he had a beginning, and thus was not eternal as God must be. As one can imagine, Arius's idea drew the attention of Church officials who were horrified that a priest could claim that Jesus was not divine, the Son of God. Such an understanding would mean that Christ's death on the cross had done nothing to atone for the original sin of Adam and Eve and the collective sin of humanity, with the consequence that humanity had not yet been redeemed. But despite the obvious contradiction between Arius's ideas and the Church's teaching that Jesus was God, many leading Church officials became allies of Arius. Why? Basically because what he said made sense logically. If the Bible said Jesus was begotten then, like all others who are begotten, there was a time when he had not existed.

This situation, which pitted Christians against each other, required resolution. Thus, in 325 CE, the Emperor Constantine, who we recall had given the "green light" for Christians to practice their faith some fourteen years earlier, called the first worldwide (or ecumenical) council of the Church to discuss this situation and provide a way forward. Thus, bishops primarily from the Eastern Mediterranean region (due in large measure to poor communication and travel opportunities at the time that prevented bishops from Western Europe from attending) met at Nicaea, in present day Turkey, to bring this controversy to a satisfactory resolution. In the process, the bishops generated the Nicene Creed, a document that clearly defined Jesus as divine and human, as well as provided some understanding of his relationship to the Father. The Creed said that Jesus was divine but also incarnate, that is, he became human. The document also described Jesus as consubstantial (in Greek, *homoousius*—"of the same substance") with the Father.

While it might seem that the situation had been resolved, unfortunately this was not the case. In fact, after the Council of Nicaea ended, Arius's theology (better known as Arianism) spread even more widely and gained more adherents. St. Jerome (347–420 CE), who gained fame through his translation of the Bible from the original Hebrew text of the Old Testament and the Greek text of the New Testament into Latin (the Vulgate), once famously wrote, "The world awoke and found itself Arian," a reference to how broadly the heresy had spread.

It was necessary, therefore, for the bishops to once again come together, this time through the effort of the Emperor Theodosius, meeting in Constantinople (modern Istanbul) in 381 CE. With the assistance of three famous Greek theologians, Sts. Basil of Caesarea, Gregory of Nyssa, and Gregory of Nazianzus (collectively known as the Cappadocian Fathers), the bishops produced a modification of the original creed, the Nicene-Constantinopolitan Creed, which continues today to be proclaimed at each Sunday and solemnity (high Church feast) Mass. They taught that God, the Trinity, had one *ousia*, what was common to all three persons and three *hypostases*, what was proper to each. Thus, God was one, but functioned as three persons—Creator (Father), Redeemer (Son), and Sanctifier (Holy Spirit).

While Arius's heresy captured the attention of the Church for over half a century, there were others who, in an attempt to better understand Jesus, also fell away from correct (literally orthodox) Church teaching. One famous example was Sabellius. He was mortified by the idea proposed by Arius that Jesus was not divine and, thus, swung the pendulum too much in the opposite direction, basically denying the humanity of Christ. In trying to explain the Trinity and Jesus's relationship with the Father and the Holy Spirit, Sabellius suggested that God at different times in history was present in various modes. During the time of Creation, God acted as the Father, the Creator, constructing the dynamic world in which we live. When the work of Creation had been completed, and humanity required redemption, then God changed modes and became a Redeemer in the person of Jesus Christ. Lastly, when Christ's work of atonement and redemption of humanity had been completed through his passion, death, and resurrection, God could once again change modes to that of sanctification, the work of the Holy Spirit, whose arrival on Pentecost Sunday we celebrate and whose abiding presence continues to fill the earth. While this seems to be a good explanation, it is a heresy, as the Church teaches that all three persons of the Trinity exist at all times; God is not manifested in different modes at various times.

The Council at Nicaea (325 CE) clearly stated that Jesus was both human and divine, while that of Constantinople (381 CE) clearly defined the Trinity. But a satisfactory explanation as to how Jesus existed both as human and divine was still lacking. Thus, Church leaders began to develop various theories as to how Jesus, the God-human, existed. From this study, two very distinct and important theological schools arose in an effort to satisfactorily explain this most important Church teaching. The first of these schools arose in Alexandria, Egypt (the home, we recall, of Arius). This Alexandrian "school" sought to protect the divinity of Christ at all costs. Its great champion, St. Cyril of Alexandria (ca. 376–449), insisted that Jesus was one person, and that he was the same before and after his incarnation in the womb of the Virgin Mary. Using the Gospel of John (primarily

1:1–18), Cyril taught that the Word (in Greek, *Logos*), the second person of the Blessed Trinity, was Jesus, the human (incarnate) Son of God. The other theological school arose in Antioch, Syria, at the time a major center of Christian thought. Seeking to protect the humanity of Jesus at all cost, proponents of this Antiochene school emphasized that Jesus had two distinct natures, one of complete divinity and one of complete humanity.

One of the great champions of the Antiochene school, Nestorius (386–451), Bishop of Constantinople, unfortunately took the basic teaching of two natures to the extreme, creating a sharp distinction between Jesus, the Son of God, and Jesus, the son of Mary. Nestorius taught that Mary was not the mother of God (in Greek, *theotokos*), but rather only the mother of the human Jesus. This was highly problematic, not so much as a slight to Mary, but more importantly what it said about Jesus. If Mary was not the mother of God, then at the time of his birth, Jesus was not God. This would necessitate that at some unknown time in his life, Jesus "became" God. This heresy, known as Adoptionism, claimed that God came upon and "adopted" Jesus, making him both human and divine. Possibly this "adoption" occurred when Jesus was found in the temple conversing with the teachers (Luke 2:41–51), or possibly when he was baptized (Matt 3:13–17), or even when he performed his first miracle (John 2:1–11). This teaching was highly problematic, for it meant that Jesus was not both human and divine from the outset.

In an effort to once again "right the ship" of the Christian faith that had drifted off course due to the teaching of Nestorius, the bishops once again came together, this time at the city of Ephesus (Turkey) in 431 CE to resolve this dispute. Cyril of Alexandria, the chief opponent of Nestorius, made certain that the bishops were called into session at the council prior to the arrival of Nestorius's supporters. Thus, the council condemned Nestorius and declared Mary to truly be the Mother of God, the *theotokos*. The heresy of Adoptionism was thus stemmed.

While one problem had been eliminated, the basic need to clearly define how Jesus was both human and divine, the work that had been inaugurated by the Alexandrian and Antiochene schools, had not been achieved. For the next twenty years, while the bishops and theologians who had been present at Ephesus had died, their disciples continued to fight the battle, leading to a final confrontation at Chalcedon (in modern Turkey) in 451 CE. One year earlier, in 450, Pope Leo I had written a famous document, known as his "Tome," which in many ways became the foundation for the bishops' teaching at Chalcedon and, thus, the Church's ultimate teaching on how Jesus was both human and divine. Leo wisely combined the teachings of both the Alexandrian and Antiochene schools in a creative way to present what has become the accepted (orthodox) teaching on how Jesus is both fully human and fully divine. Drawing from the divinity side of the Alexandrian school, Leo taught that Jesus was always one person, before and after the incarnation. From the Antiochene School and its teaching on the humanity of Christ, Leo taught that this one person was present in two natures. He emphasized that the humanity of Jesus was derived from the flesh of Mary, and his divinity from the Holy Spirit. These two natures were totally intertwined; there could be no separation.

When the bishops met one year after Leo's "Tome," their work was greatly simplified. They basically followed the teaching of the "Tome," placing it in more formal language. The exact definition is, however, important and thus should be stated as it was originally presented:

> Therefore, following the holy Fathers, we all with one accord teach men to acknowledge one and the same Son, our Lord Jesus Christ, at once complete in Godhead and complete in manhood, truly God and truly man, consisting also of a reasonable soul and body; of one substance with the Father as regards his Godhead,

and at the same time of one substance with us as regards his manhood; like us in all respects, apart from sin; as regards his Godhead, begotten of the Father before the ages, but yet as regards his manhood begotten, for us men and for our salvation, of Mary the Virgin, the God-bearer; one in the same Christ, Son, Lord, Only-begotten, recognized in two natures, without confusion, without change, without division, without separation; the distinction of natures being in no way annulled by the union, but rather the characteristics of each nature being preserved and coming together to form one person and subsistence, not as parted or separated into two persons, but one and the same Son and Only-begotten God the Word, Lord Jesus Christ; even as the prophets from earliest times spoke of him and our Lord Jesus Christ himself taught us and the Creed of the Fathers has handed down to us.[1]

THE SIGNIFICANCE OF THE CHURCH'S TEACHING

Our investigation into the basic question of Matthew 16:15 ("Who do you say that I am?") must begin formally with the common understanding of the specific doctrine of the Church. As explained above, these teachings were not understood and articulated at the time of Jesus. Christ did not provide his followers with either a blueprint on how to understand God as a unity of three persons in one God, nor how Jesus could be both fully human and divine at the same time. There was no road map to follow. Thus, it was essential for our ancestors in the faith to define the true and proper understanding of God and his Son,

Jesus. It is equally important for us who live some two thousand years later to have a clear and unambiguous understanding of these fundamental questions of our faith. The struggles that men and women of faith endured in order to understand the complexity of God are, fortunately for us, not our concern. Rather, our challenge is to use the teachings we have been given, and the understanding of God that they give us, to draw closer to Christ and to apply the teachings he left, as articulated in the Scriptures, in ways that benefit the common good, and by that means assist ourselves in the daily journey of walking with the Lord and being his contemporary disciples.

CONCLUSION

Having an appreciation for and knowledge of the development of the Church's teaching on Jesus can assist us in answering who Jesus is for us today. Our investigation has begun by building the foundation, one might say a general framework, upon which we can construct, brick-by-brick, the building that will be our personal understanding of Jesus. In efforts to understand Jesus and his relationship to the Father and Holy Spirit, some, like Arius, Sabellius, and Nestorius, drew heretical conclusions. Thus, it was necessary to inaugurate the worldwide or ecumenical councils to clearly and definitively define the dogmas of the Trinity and the reality of Jesus as simultaneously both human and divine.

These Church teachings are critical to our understanding as we initiate in a formal way our investigation of Jesus's classic question to Peter. While, as we will see through this inquiry, there are many ideas, models, and various perspectives that will determine how we understand Jesus, the rock and foundation, specifically what the Church teaches about Jesus will be the same. This is the common foundation for our investigation, but the height, breadth, and construction of who Jesus is will be up to you, the reader.

Discussion Questions

1. In your opinion, what were the most important factors that prompted early Christians to seek answers about God and Jesus? Were things like Christianity's minority status or the persecutions significant, or was it simpler, such as basic human curiosity?
2. Why do you believe it took so long, and was such a severe struggle, for early Christians to clearly define God and Jesus Christ?
3. How does the Church's teaching that Jesus is eternally both totally human and divine influence how you answer Jesus's question of "Who do you say that I am?"
4. Today it is easy to say that people like Arius and Nestorius were wrong and should be labeled as heretics. However, if you could put yourself in the situation that these men (and others) experienced, would your reaction be different? Do you find the "explanations" of those labeled heretics to have any reasonable justification?
5. At the outset of our investigation of who Jesus is, do you relate more to his humanity or divinity? Why?

Chapter 3

JESUS OF THE SCRIPTURES

Christian theologians use the term *revelation* when describing how God is revealed to humanity. Catholicism quite clearly teaches, and Vatican II verified in 1963 with *Sacrosanctum Concilium* (The Constitution on the Sacred Liturgy), that there is one source of revelation, but this source has three component parts: Scripture, Sacred Tradition, and the teaching office of the Church, the Magisterium. Throughout the Common Era, when seeking to answer various religious questions, Christians have always started the process by looking at revelation and its most basic component, the Bible. Thus, the question that this book seeks to answer, "Who do you say that I am?" necessitates a thorough and close examination of what Scripture says about Jesus. Of the twenty-seven books that comprise the New Testament, the four Gospels (namely Matthew, Mark, Luke, and John) are, for the study of Jesus, primary. Certainly, the letters of St. Paul and the other books of the New Testament testify in varied ways about Jesus and, especially in the case of Paul, provide sound theology that has guided Christian thought for two thousand years. It is the Gospels, however, that provide the greatest insight, for they describe the life, mission, and message of Jesus. Ascribed, we are told by scholars, by two men who knew Jesus intimately (Matthew and John), and two others (Mark and Luke) who were contemporaries of Christ, these documents of faith provide the Christian community the raw information of what Jesus did, where he went, what he said, and how his message was received by those to whom it was proclaimed. The Scriptures, therefore, provide a basic building block in our quest to answer the question Jesus posed to the apostles: "Who do you say that I am?"

THE GOSPELS: GENERAL INFORMATION

In order to understand what the Scriptures say about Jesus, it is essential to understand the basics behind the gospel tradition. The word *Gospel* is taken from the Greek term *euangelion*, which translates as "good news." Indeed, for Christians, the four Gospels are the good news, for they provide the most complete historical and theological understanding of Jesus Christ, the founder and central figure of our faith. Why, we might ask, did our ancestors in the faith feel a need to provide a written account of the life and mission of Jesus? Originally Christians, like all groups, generated an oral tradition that served to pass along the events of Jesus's life, and the meaning of his mission to the world. However, this oral tradition, like a family tradition, needed to be communicated to different peoples and to be safeguarded. Therefore, approximately one generation after the death and resurrection of Christ, his followers began to write down what they had heard and personally witnessed during the life, and especially the public ministry, of Jesus.

It is very important to understand that the Gospels were

not written with the intention of historical accuracy as we understand it today. When we read a history book, we generally assume that the dates, places, and events narrated are precisely as they happened historically. The Gospels were never intended to be documents of this nature. Rather, these texts were written by specific people at specific times to a specific community, seeking to present not only the historical reality but the mission and message of Christ in a way that could be understood by the community addressed. In other words, the Gospels were not intended to be biographies of Jesus. This reality helps to explain why there are so many differences and inconsistencies among the Gospels as we read them. For example, Matthew and Luke provide important information about the birth and early years of Jesus, but Mark and John do not even mention these events. Why, when reading about similar historical events, such as the Last Supper and the resurrection, do the accounts of the evangelists differ? This is not to say, in any way, that the Gospels are not presenting the historical reality of Jesus, but rather to help us understand why different Gospels present different events (e.g., St. John is the only one who mentions Jesus washing the feet of his disciples at the Last Supper) and how similar events are narrated in different ways with varied details. The evangelists did not seek to relate all that Jesus did, and since we have no written record of anything composed by the Lord himself, we are relying totally on the observations and memory of others. The introduction to the Constitution on Divine Revelation (*Dei Verbum*), one of sixteen documents to emerge from Vatican II, summarizes what the Church teaches about the Gospels in a very readable format:

> Holy Mother Church has firmly and with absolute constancy held, and continues to hold, that the four Gospels...whose historical character the Church unhesitatingly asserts, faithfully hand on what Jesus Christ, while living among men, really did and taught

> for their eternal salvation, until the day he was taken up into heaven. (para. 19)

How were the Gospels composed? First, we must understand that they were written over time. The evangelists, either from personal memory or from knowledge obtained from others who actually walked with the Lord, took his words as the base for their writing. The aforementioned oral tradition that circulated about the events, especially the miracles and teaching of Jesus, were also a central source for these writers. Lastly, and importantly, each of the evangelists has in his Gospel certain events that are unique to the particular evangelist. For example, the famous parables of the prodigal son and the Good Samaritan are found only in the Gospel of Luke (15:11–32 and 10:25–37, respectively). Jesus's first miracle to change water into wine is only in John's Gospel (2:1–11).

Another important question to ask is why these were the four Gospels included in the New Testament, when there are other documents that also claimed to be gospel literature. This excellent question can be answered by addressing some of the criteria used by the Church over Christian history to determine which documents of faith have actually been included in the thirty-nine books of the Old Testament[1] and the twenty-seven books of the New Testament. The first criterion is apostolic origin; in other words, who wrote it? Was the apparent author someone who personally knew or walked with Jesus during his earthly life? While this is not certain confirmation that a document written by someone who claims the name of an apostle or other disciple of Jesus is actually authentic Scripture, it does give at least one possible indication of its validity. Next, scholars ask who was the community being addressed; to whom was the document written. If the recipient community was a group of people known in the region and at the time, then again, while not convincing, it adds more evidence to the document's validity.

Third, and very importantly, did the document conform to the rule of faith? In other words, what did it say? Are there ideas in the text that are completely inconsistent, based on other known data, with the life and mission of Jesus Christ? A good example of conformity to the rule of faith is found in the Gnostic Gospel of Thomas. Thomas was certainly one of the twelve apostles and the text addresses the early Christian community, but in several places its teachings are quite contrary to those of Jesus. For example, the very end of this Gospel reads, "Simon Peter said to them, 'Let Mary leave us, because women are not worthy of life.' Jesus said, 'Behold, I shall guide her so as to make her male, that she too may become a living spirit like you men. For every woman who makes herself male will enter the kingdom of heaven.'" Clearly, this passage is totally inconsistent with Jesus's message of inclusion. The final two criteria used by scholars to determine the validity of early Christian texts were popular use and chance. Was any particular document being utilized by the early Christian community in its worship? If yes, then this would add evidence to its validity. In some cases, however, such as the letters of St. Ignatius of Antioch (ca. 35–107) or the writings of St. Clement (?–99), one of the first-century popes, all the criteria seem to have been met, and thus the question, "Why are they not part of the Bible?" It simply seems that by chance they were not included in the New Testament.

THE SYNOPTIC GOSPELS

The four canonical Gospels (those in the New Testament) are divided into two groups: the Synoptics (Matthew, Mark, and Luke) and John. The Synoptics are grouped together for several different reasons. First, all three suggest that the public ministry of Jesus was one year in length. How was this determined? Scholars suggest that faithful Jewish males, which certainly included

Jesus, would have made every effort to go to Jerusalem for the annual celebration of Passover. In the Synoptics, Jesus travels to Jerusalem only once, when he ultimately undergoes his passion, death, and resurrection. Thus, the conclusion is that his public ministry lasted one year. All three of the Synoptics have many similar stories in their narratives and sources in their composition. Some familiar stories contained in all three of these Gospels are the baptism of Jesus, his temptation in the desert before the initiation of his public ministry, the healing of Peter's mother-in-law, the healings of the paralytic, the transfiguration, the call of Levi (Matthew), several important parables, such as the sower and the mustard seed, and a number of miracles, such as the healing of Bartimaeus and the epileptic boy, and the feeding of the five thousand. Finally, the Synoptics had certain common sources, especially Matthew and Luke.

For many generations, scholars believed that the Gospel of Matthew, because of its length, was the first to be written, but more contemporary biblical experts tell us that the first Gospel chronologically is Mark. While we have no copyright date, as is customary with any contemporary book, scholars today suggest that this first Gospel was written approximately in the year 65 CE, some thirty-five years after the death and resurrection of Jesus. Who is the author? Since the name Mark is not among the twelve apostles, we must look elsewhere for an answer. The Acts of the Apostles (12:12, 25; 15:37) speaks of one "John Mark" who was a companion of Paul in his travels through the Eastern Mediterranean world. The letters of St. Paul, specifically Colossians 4:10, 2 Timothy 4:11, and Philemon 1:24, also referred to a man named Mark. The Gospel of Mark itself (14:52) speaks of a man who, while observing the arrest of Jesus, "left the linen cloth and ran off naked." Some scholars suggest the evangelist is speaking of himself. If this is the case, then although not an apostle, clearly he was one of the many unnamed disciples of Jesus. Mark's Gospel is addressed to non-Jewish Christians, namely Gentiles who had converted to Christianity, most probably beyond the borders of Israel. The primary sources for Mark's Gospel are an Aramaic-language version of a Gospel attributed to Matthew and the evangelist's own information, including, of course, the oral history and tradition that circulated about Jesus.[2]

Written on the heels of Mark is the Gospel of Luke. Biblical scholars believe that this text was written approximately during the years 70 to 75 by Luke, the same person who penned the Acts of the Apostles. Luke was not one of the original twelve, but did accompany St. Paul on some of his missionary trips. This background would clearly indicate why scholars say that this Gospel was addressed to Gentile Christians, non-Jews who had converted to the New Way (Christianity). The nature of his audience dictated that Luke not use terminology or refer to places that only Jews would know and understand. The evangelist's sources were the Gospel of Mark, Luke's own particular material, for example as mentioned above, the parables of the Good Samaritan and the prodigal son, and a third new source, referred to as the "Q source."[3]

The third, chronologically last, but longest of the three Synoptic Gospels is Matthew. Written approximately in the year 85 CE, after the destruction of the temple by the Romans in the year 70, the Gospel's authorship is attributed to Matthew (also known as Levi), one of the twelve original apostles. His audience was primarily Aramaic-speaking Jewish converts in Palestine. Matthew also used the Gospel of Mark and "Q," as well as his own specific input, in the composition of this text.

Now that we have a basic understanding of the Synoptic tradition, we should look at one of the most basic elements that is common to all of these Gospels, Jesus's use of parables. What precisely is a parable? A good basic definition would be a story that conveys a lesson with a double meaning, the literal meaning of the story and a deeper and more profound message. Parables were used to effect change in those who heard them, leading to some moral decision or action. Thus, parables have three important points:

- They are narratives generally of a popular or folk nature.
- The stories are on two levels—a literal and deeper moral message.
- Parables are more than entertainment; they convey an ethical or religious message.

Why did Jesus use the vehicle of parables? One can imagine that the message of Jesus, which was so countercultural and challenging to the people of his day, would not be popular with many. Thus, first, parables could be used to conceal his teaching to outsiders, while revealing his message to his disciples. Second, parables were used to disarm his listeners. There is no better example of this than the parable of the Good Samaritan. Jesus challenged the religious elite to choose compassion over strict adherence to the Mosaic Law by portraying someone like a Samaritan, a member of one of the most despised groups in Israel during Jesus's time, as a hero while a priest and Levite, members of the Jewish religious elite, were painted as villains. People were certainly taken aback; they were disarmed. Lastly, and possibly most importantly, the vehicle of parables makes Jesus's teaching timeless. The messages presented in these parables, while being understood in different ways by different people, have always been and always will be applicable to society. Their message is indeed timeless.

THE GOSPEL OF JOHN

The Synoptic tradition of the New Testament is complemented by the Gospel of John. The New Testament actually has five books attributed to an author named John—the Gospel, three letters of John, and the Book of Revelation. Who are the authors of these important New Testament texts? Analysis of these five books by biblical scholars reveals a significant difference in the words used by the authors. Research has shown that the Book of Revelation is written in a more popular, one might say lower level, of Greek, the original language of the New Testament. The other four books, the Gospel and the three letters attributed to John, on the other hand, are written in a more scholarly, one might say higher level, of Greek. Hence the conclusion is reached that since the apostle John was, as we read in the Gospels themselves, a fisherman and, thus, most probably not privileged with an advanced education,[4] he is the author of Revelation. Some disciple of John is most likely the author of the Gospel and three letters. Scholars suggest that this Gospel was written in the late first century and addressed to Christians living outside Palestine.

Besides authorship, the Gospel of John is unique in several ways, and thus stands apart from the Synoptic tradition. Possibly most importantly, the author of John's Gospel presumes that the reader is familiar with the information, stories, and so on in the Synoptics. Therefore, there is no need to restate information the reader already knows. Thus, John does not speak of Jesus's birth or childhood (for that matter neither does Mark), and says nothing about the institution of the Eucharist at the Last Supper. While this Gospel does not describe certain important aspects of Jesus's life, it does include other important details not found in the Synoptics. Jesus's first miracle at Cana, his highly theological discussion on the bread of life (chapter 6), and the story of Jesus washing the feet of his disciples at the Last Supper are three examples. Unlike the Synoptics, John narrates a three-year (not a one-year) public ministry of Jesus. As described above, this is determined by how many times Jesus goes to Jerusalem in the narrative. John's Gospel has no parables. It does have allegory, such as the popular metaphor in which he compares himself with his disciples as a grapevine to its branches. The Gospel of John is also highly symbolic. When reading the text, references to the Blessed Virgin Mary are understood by scholars to be a symbol of the Church. The famous "I am" statements where Jesus calls himself bread, light, shepherd, and so on, are also symbolic.[5]

HOW DO THE SCRIPTURES DESCRIBE JESUS?

With a solid background on the Gospels, including authorship, date of composition, sources, and some common and unique aspects of these four books of the New Testament, we can now look at the various ways Jesus is presented in the Gospels. If contemporaries of the Lord had been asked, "Who is Jesus?" several responses would have been received. In the Jewish tradition he would certainly have been seen as a prophet. While the Hebrew prophets of old (Isaiah, Jeremiah, Amos, Hosea, etc.) did speak of future events, their primary mission was to speak of the ills of society during their time and to call for reform. For example, Isaiah warned the people in the Southern Kingdom of Judah that if they did not reform, their fate would be similar to that of their neighbors to the north, Israel, which had been overrun and destroyed by the Assyrians in 722 BCE. Similarly, Amos warned the religious elite of the Hebrews that if they did not reform their oppressive tactics against the poor in the land, disaster would strike. In a similar way, Jesus addressed the scribes and Pharisees, challenging them to change their ways and demonstrate greater compassion toward others. Thus, clearly Jesus was a prophet in the line of men like Isaiah and Amos.

The title "prophet" certainly describes Jesus, but so too the label "teacher." Jesus was the greatest of teachers. Every word from his mouth and every action of his life were purposeful in seeking to teach his followers a new way of life. As the Lord said, "Do not think that I have come to abolish the law or the prophets; I have come not to abolish but to fulfill" (Matt 5:17). The parables, the Sermon on the Mount, and his prayers were significant teaching moments. The same can be said for the miracles he performed. Through these miracles, Jesus could also claim the title of "healer," for he indeed cured both body and soul. He was also a reconciler, whether it was the woman of Samaria (John 4:1–42), the woman caught in adultery (John 8:2–11), the good thief on the cross (Luke 23:42–43), or even Peter, helping him to reconcile with Christ after his three denials (John 18:15–27).

What were the roles that Jesus fulfilled as described in the Scriptures; how did he describe his purpose? While Jesus only once positively acknowledged that he was the Messiah (Mark 14:61–62), this title was in many ways the presumption of the Jewish people who followed him. While he did not fit the description presented in Jeremiah 23:5–6 of a kingly person who would restore Israel to its previous greatness, he certainly did fit quite closely the description of the Messiah presented in the four Suffering Servant passages found in Isaiah (42:1–4; 49:1–6; 50:4–8; 52:13—53:12). Through the paschal mystery, his passion, death, and resurrection, Jesus fulfills the role of Redeemer. St. Paul put it well: "Therefore just as one man's trespass led to condemnation for all, so one man's act of righteousness leads to justification and life for all" (Rom 5:18). Jesus's courageous act of self-sacrifice was his atonement for the original sin of Adam and Eve, placing humanity on the road that could lead to salvation.

Possibly the most visible role of Jesus as portrayed in the Gospels is that of miracle worker. In his first publicly recorded statement in the synagogue of his hometown of Nazareth, Jesus proclaimed,

> The Spirit of the Lord is upon me,
> because he has anointed me
> to bring good news to the poor.
> He has sent me to proclaim release to the captives
> and recovery of sight to the blind,
> to let the oppressed go free,
> to proclaim the year of the Lord's favor. (Luke 4:18–19)

Jesus brought the good news through proclamations, but also through the curing of the destitute—lepers (Mark 1:40–45), the crazed Legion (Mark 5:1–20), and the woman with a hemorrhage (Mark 5:25–34)—and raising the dead to life (Luke 7:11–17; John 11:1–44). By such action he brought good news to others. Not only did he restore the physical sight of the blind, like Bartimaeus (Mark 10:46–52), but possibly more importantly cured the spiritual blindness that was present with many, including the man born blind (John 9:1–41). Additionally, Jesus's ability to control the weather (e.g., Mark 4:35–41) marked him as a miracle worker in a very profound way. Lastly, Jesus was one who reached out in a preferential way to those who are oppressed. He held an important conversation with a Samaritan woman and in his famous parable declared the Good Samaritan to be a hero. He had no problem freely associating with the lowly in Hebrew society and even going beyond the confines of Israel, visiting Tyre, Sidon, and the region of the Decapolis (Mark 7:31).

CONCLUSION

The Scriptures, especially the four Gospels, provide us with much information in our quest to answer Jesus's basic question: "Who do you say that I am?" Different accounts presented by the evangelists provide much information about Jesus, helping us to understand his significant roles in Hebrew society. The many titles and roles that Jesus fulfilled during his earthly life allow one to apply the Scriptures to the question of our quest in different ways. For some, Jesus will be the greatest teacher; for others, he will be one who brought us redemption. Still others will see him as a model for life, as a miracle worker and one who reached out to those in need. Equipped with this additional information, we can look at other important aspects of the Lord's life, continuing to seek the answer to Jesus's question: "Who do you say that I am?"

Discussion Questions

1. Which of the four Gospels do you find most attractive or beneficial for your spiritual life? Why would you choose this particular Gospel?
2. Does the fact that the Gospels were written as documents of faith for people of faith, rather than a "biography" of Jesus, present a challenge to you? Does this fact help you to better understand the Gospels themselves?
3. Which of the parables of Jesus do you find most comforting; which do you find the most challenging? Why?
4. To which of the many roles of Jesus can you best relate? Why?
5. If you were asked what the central message of the Gospels is, how would you answer?

Chapter 4

JESUS OF FAITH

In chapter 1 of our investigation, we explored the basic question, "Who is Jesus?" and we were introduced to the work of Scripture scholar Marcus Borg. Two paradigms of Jesus were presented, the earlier, which stressed faith in Christ, and the emerging, which placed greater emphasis on the historical Jesus. The earlier paradigm has historically been the dominant one, as it views Jesus from the perspective of his resurrection. Christ is seen in this paradigm as the divine being in whom we must place our trust and faith. Having explored the development of the Church's teaching on Jesus, and having an appreciation of how he is portrayed in the Scriptures, we can now investigate a basic response to our question, "Who do you say that I am?" For most people the instant, almost instinctual, even reflex answer is that Jesus is the resurrected Savior, the one in whom the average Christian's faith is centered. Yet, there is much more to this basic response. How did Jesus understand himself? What were the titles that contemporaries of Jesus used when addressing him? What do the events of Jesus's life tell us about him as the one in whom we should place our faith? These are the basic questions we will now raise.

THE PERSON OF JESUS

How did Jesus understand God; how did he call upon God? As a practicing Jewish man, one could readily expect Jesus to relate to God in a very personable way. While Yahweh is depicted in the Hebrew Bible (what Christians normally refer to as the Old Testament) as a powerful force, exacting punishment for sin but also manifesting compassion, this Jewish understanding was radically different than other polytheistic societies who occupied the same general area of the world. For example, the Greeks spoke of an inanimate unmoved mover as the cause of all that existed. Jesus, more like his Jewish roots, saw God as a person. The most frequent term used by Jesus in the New Testament when referring to God is *Father* (used sixty-five times in the Synoptics and over one hundred times in the Gospel of John.) In Mark's Gospel and the letters of St. Paul, the Aramaic word *Abba*, generally translated as "daddy," is used by Jesus when referring to God. Thus, Jesus addresses God in a very personable, warm, and tender way, expressing even a unique intimacy with God. The word *Abba* is also used by St. Paul in Romans 8:15 and Galatians 4:6, which indicates that the early Church fully understood the unique intimacy, warmth, and tenderness of the relationship between Jesus and the Father.

Jesus saw God as a person, one with whom he could speak on an intimate basis, but how did the Lord understand himself; what was the personhood of Jesus? More than any other title, Jesus referred to himself as the Son of Man, using this title in three different ways. First, he used the term *Son of Man* when referring to his second coming, which theologians call the *Parousia*. For example, Mark 13:24–27 reads,

> But in those days, after that suffering,
> the sun will be darkened,
>   and the moon will not give its light,
> and the stars will be falling from heaven,
>   and the powers in the heavens will be shaken.
>
> Then they will see "the Son of Man coming in clouds" with great power and glory. Then he will send out the angels, and gather his elect from the four winds, from the ends of the earth to the ends of heaven.

Next, Jesus used this title when speaking of his ministry during his earthly life. Mark 2:10–11 illustrates this idea: "'But so that you may know that the Son of Man has authority on earth to forgive sins'—he said to the paralytic—'I say to you, stand up, take your mat and go to your home.'" Lastly, Jesus called himself Son of Man in reference to his future suffering and resurrection. In Mark 10:45 we read, "For the Son of Man came not to be served but to serve, and to give his life a ransom for many."

A second title that Jesus used for himself was Son of God. For centuries Christians surely understood this to mean that Jesus was claiming he was God, but this is not necessarily the case. We must understand that the term *Son of God* was broadly used in the ancient Near East, referring not to an eternal being, but rather as an expression of honor and respect. Additionally, many Jews saw Israel metaphorically as God's firstborn son. So it was easy for Jesus to translate this expression and appropriate it for himself. While most people might instinctively think that Jesus would have called himself the Messiah, for indeed he was the long-expected messenger, Christ never used this expression for himself. Only on one occasion did he acknowledge, when questioned, that he was the Messiah (Mark 14:61–62).

Possibly the most interesting way that Jesus identified himself was through his series of seven "I am" statements in the

Gospel of John. As explained earlier in chapter 1, Jesus claims he is "the bread of life" (6:48), "the light of the world (8:12), "the gate for the sheep" (10:7), "the good shepherd" (10:11), "the resurrection and the life" (11:25), "the way, and the truth, and the life" (14:6), and "the true vine" (15:1). Faithful Jews would have made the connection with Moses's encounter with Yahweh (Exod 3:14) when the latter called himself "I AM WHO I AM."

Jesus's understanding of God, and of himself, must be balanced with a short analysis of the titles others gave to him. In response to Jesus's original question, "Who do people say that the Son of Man is?" (Matt 16:13), the apostles invoke historical people, specifically John the Baptist, Elijah, and Jeremiah. Thus, at this point Jesus is seen as a normal human being, greatly respected, but not in any way divine. However, when Peter responds to Jesus's second question, "Who do you say that I am?" the question of our inquiry, he invokes the divine nature of Jesus, referring to him as "the Messiah, the Son of the living God" (Matt 16:16). The Jesus of faith thus begins to emerge.

ACTIONS OF JESUS

Peter's confession of faith does not, however, "come out of nowhere." It rather arises through a process of development. This evolution begins when Jesus first calls Peter to be an apostle. St. Luke narrates a powerful story of how Jesus used Peter's boat as a platform to teach the crowds. When he concluded his teaching, he told Peter, "Put out into the deep water and let down your nets for a catch" (5:4). Although Peter initially protested, saying that he and his companions had worked hard all night and had not been successful, in the end he does as Jesus requests. When they catch so many fish that their nets are at the point of breaking, Peter is overwhelmed and falls on his knees in front of Jesus exclaiming, "Go away from me, Lord, for I am a sinful man!" (Luke 5:8). Indeed, Peter's amazement is so great that he refers to Jesus as "Lord," indicating from the very outset of their relationship that the chosen head of the apostles (and later the Church) understood that Jesus was special and probably more than a mere human being. This same phenomenon of recognition was expressed by all the apostles sometime later. St. Matthew (14:22–33) tells the story of Jesus walking on the water and inviting Peter to join him. Initially Peter is fine, but when he realizes what he is doing, his fear clouds his faith and he falters. Eventually, Jesus rescues Peter and calms the storm. This prompts the other eleven in the boat to profess, "Truly you are the Son of God" (Matt 14:33).

The profession of Peter itself is described by all three Synoptic evangelists: Matthew 16:13–23; Mark 8:27–33; and Luke 9:18–22. There are many similarities in these three accounts, but there are also some differences. All three evangelists report that these events happened in the region of Caesarea Philippi. In response to Jesus's initial question, all three offer the names of John the Baptist and Elijah as answers; all three also more generically state that others see Jesus as "one of the prophets." In response to Jesus's second question, "Who do you say that I am?" all three evangelists also credit Peter with proclaiming that Jesus is the Messiah. Lastly, all three of the Gospel evangelists predict the future suffering of Jesus. Differences arise mostly in detail and a few small nuances. Matthew is the only text that has Peter profess Jesus to be the "Son of the living God." Most importantly, however, this famous incident in the life of Jesus depicts how Peter moved from seeing Jesus as a mere human, a man of history, to a divine figure, a man of faith.

Besides the famous profession of faith, the transfiguration of Jesus, also narrated by all three Synoptic writers (Matt 17:1–8; Mark 9:2–8; Luke 9:28–36) is crucial to our understanding of Jesus as a person of faith. As with the aforementioned profession of Peter, both similarities and differences are present with the three accounts of this miraculous vision. All three writers say that these events occurred on a high mountain, that the event was witnessed by Peter, James, and John, and that Jesus's appearance was altered in some way (Matthew and Mark use the specific word "transfigured"). All three writers also speak of Jesus being present with Moses and Elijah and, as the vision continued, a cloud came overhead and a voice from the cloud proclaimed, "This is my Son…listen to him." Differences exist in the detail provided by Luke concerning the number of days after Peter's profession of faith (six versus eight) that these events occurred.

A direct connection is made by all of the evangelists between Peter's confession and Jesus's transfiguration. First, Peter's confession that Jesus is indeed divine is verified by the vision of the transfiguration. Jesus physically proves his divinity immediately after his chosen leader has professed this same reality. A second link is made between the future crucifixion of Jesus and his glorification. As the Lord predicts his future suffering during the profession of Peter, he shows that he will then be glorified through the image of his transfiguration. The two events so linked challenge the apostles and, by extension, all of us, to raise our spiritual selves, to both inwardly and outwardly ascend to the greater heights to which Christ calls us.

Unquestionably, the story of Jesus's resurrection, described in all four of the Gospels, provides the greatest evidence to the "Jesus of faith" model. As the central event in Christian history, the resurrection, for many centuries, and even today for most Christians, provides the perspective, one might say the lens, through which Jesus is seen and understood. Without the resurrection, the story of Jesus would be a simple note in history. St. Paul makes this crystal clear when writing to the Christian community at Corinth:

> If the dead are not raised, then Christ has not been raised. If Christ has not been raised, your faith is

> futile and you are still in your sins. Then those also who have died in Christ have perished. If for this life only we have hoped in Christ, we are of all people most to be pitied. (1 Cor 15:16–19)

The Jesus of faith sees Christ as this resurrected Savior, the one who has conquered death for all people for all time and, through his passion, death, and resurrection, brought the possibility of eternal life to all who believe. This perspective is only possible through the reality of the resurrection.

What does Christianity claim in the resurrection of Jesus? First, it is assumed that the tomb in which Jesus was buried was empty and this was so because God raised him from death. It is also claimed that after the resurrection, Jesus appeared to his followers on a few occasions in a form that could be seen, heard, and touched. In other words, Jesus was bodily raised from the dead.

We might ask, what did these events mean to those first followers of Jesus? While the apostles and early disciples of Jesus were certainly euphoric that their great champion, the one whom they had followed from the beginning of his public ministry, was alive, somehow conquering death, the resurrection meant so much more. The earlier profession of Peter, the vision of the transfiguration, and the other events witnessed by these followers of the Lord, was now verified. From this time forward there was no way to ever "see" or understand Jesus then as a resurrected Savior. All of his words and actions would henceforth be seen through this very specific lens. This perspective would stand the test of time and be the foundation upon which the life and mission of Christ would be spread throughout the world. As described in chapter 1, Marcus Borg's earlier paradigm, the Jesus of faith, began with the personal experience of those who walked the road with Jesus and continued over the centuries through the gospel tradition as recorded by the four evangelists.

What precisely do the resurrection accounts tell us? The original (shorter) version of Mark's Gospel, which ends at 16:8, only says that Jesus was raised; we have no other information. The longer version, ending at 16:20, speaks of his appearances to Mary Magdalene and two unnamed disciples; it ends with his ascension. The other three Gospels, Matthew, Luke, and John, all present various stories of Jesus appearing to those who had been his followers. St. Matthew describes Jesus's encounter with Mary Magdalene and his commissioning of the eleven apostles, commanding them to go forth and baptize and make disciples of all nations (Matt 28:1–10, 16–20). St. Luke also reports Jesus's appearance to Mary Magdalene, but adds two others who were in her company, Joanna and Mary the mother of James (Luke 24:1–12). Luke also presents the famous Emmaus story, when Jesus walked with Cleopas and a second unnamed disciple, explaining passages in Scripture that spoke of his life, and ultimately revealing his identity, then disappearing from their sight while breaking the bread (Luke 24:13–35). Later, Luke reports how Jesus appeared to all of the apostles. St. John also presents the Mary Magdalene story (20:11–18) but precedes that with the discovery by Peter and John that the Lord is not in his tomb. John gives us two additional post-resurrection accounts, that of "Doubting Thomas" (John 20:24–29) and a special conversation between Jesus and Peter (21:1–25) that allowed the chosen head of the apostles to profess three affirmations of faith in the Lord, countering his three denials in the early morning of Good Friday. Clearly the disciples of Jesus had experiences of him after death that convinced them that he was with them in the present moment.

What do these accounts collectively say about Jesus? Interestingly, Jesus demonstrates both human and divine attributes after the resurrection. He eats fish, a common, ordinary food, but he also passes through doors that are locked and disappears. One very interesting common denominator is that those whom

Jesus knew best do not seem to recognize him in his resurrected state. Mary Magdalene thinks he is the gardener; the disciples on the way to Emmaus had no idea who he was. Even the apostles think they have seen a ghost when he appears to them in the upper room. Why, one might ask, did those who knew him best not recognize him? On a practical level, one might answer that these people were so shocked and saddened by Jesus's death that viewing him in a resurrected state would be shocking, even inconceivable. Another answer might be that Jesus's resurrected appearance was indeed different than before his death. Certainly, many other answers could be offered, but one associated with the model of the Jesus of faith suggests that Christ wanted others to recognize his presence in the faces, words, and actions of others. Jesus wanted people to see him through the eyes of faith.

The Jesus of faith model is also readily manifest in the life of St. Paul. As the Acts of the Apostles (9:1–19) describes, Jesus appeared as a resurrected Savior to Paul. This transformative moment in Paul's life convinced him that Jesus was indeed alive. This could only happen, however, through the eyes of faith. Jesus had conquered death; he was not simply a historical figure, but rather for Paul and all to whom he would preach, a subject of faith. Paul realized the significance of Jesus as a resurrected Savior. The resurrection was the event that made Christianity possible; it was the catalyst to the concept of the Jesus of faith.

CONCLUSION

Exploring the idea of the Jesus of faith adds greatly to our complement of tools that can be used to answer Jesus's great question: "Who do you say that I am?" Most people are very comfortable, both historically and even today, with the view that Jesus was indeed the resurrected Savior, the one who had been promised, the Messiah. Thus, to such people the miracles and various teachings of Jesus are not a stretch, but rather something that could simply be expected from a divine being who had risen from the dead. There is no need to question the historical reality of Jesus; faith does not depend on historical knowledge. The rapid and broad expanse of Christianity testifies to the faith of the millions through the centuries who have followed Jesus. The challenge for people in today's post-Enlightenment world, who demand scientific proof and/or verifiable evidence for any belief, is to continue their witness that Jesus is Lord, the resurrected Savior, whose life and mission continue to inspire men and women of faith.

Discussion Questions

1. What role does faith in Christ play in your life? Is your faith in Jesus central, or is it one of many aspects of your day-to-day existence?
2. Pope Emeritus Benedict XVI once wrote, "Where is the post-Easter faith supposed to come from if Jesus made no foundation for it before Easter?" How do you react to this question?
3. Which event in Jesus's life do you see as central to the Jesus of faith paradigm?
4. Why, in your opinion, did those who knew Jesus best not recognize him after the resurrection? Was Jesus trying to send a message to them and, by extension, all who would follow after them?
5. How does the Jesus of faith paradigm assist you in answering our question, "Who do you say that I am?"

Chapter 5

CHRIST OF HISTORY

Since the time Jesus walked the earth, Christians have viewed him and taught others to understand him as the Son of God, the Redeemer who performed miracles and taught us how to live through word and deed. The basic "assumption" that the events recorded in the Gospels were precise historical realities as they are narrated was accepted by all. The reason that Jesus could raise the dead, walk on water, and control the weather was that he was the resurrected Savior, the divine second person of the Blessed Trinity.

The intellectual advances achieved through the Scientific Revolution and the Enlightenment of the seventeenth and eighteenth centuries prompted, among other things, a new look at Jesus. Scholars began to ask questions about the historical reality of the Scriptures. Were they true historical narratives, or were they simply stories put together by people of faith to convince others of their specific understanding of Jesus as the divine Son of God? Scientific evidence that began to prove centuries-long beliefs on the solar system to be inaccurate became the catalyst that drove some to seek similar concrete confirmation that Jesus actually acted and spoke as narrated by the four evangelists. Was there sufficient evidence, some began to assert, to know for certain that Jesus not only walked the earth, but more importantly, performed the actions and spoke the words that are the inspiration behind the faith of billions of Christians who have followed Christ's teachings over the centuries?

Examining the Christ of history, what Marcus Borg described in an earlier chapter as the "emerging paradigm," must, therefore, be the next step in answering the Lord's question to Peter: "Who do you say that I am?" We will find challenges to the "earlier paradigm" but also much evidence that verifies that the Jesus of faith and the Jesus of history are indeed one.

WHAT DOES HISTORY TELL US ABOUT JESUS?

While not abundant, there are some important secular historians and philosophers from antiquity who refer to a "Christ" figure in first-century Palestine. The first-century Jewish historian Flavius Josephus (37–100) speaks of a certain Christus, founder of the "new way," that is the Christian community, who was executed by the order of Pontius Pilate. The Roman historian Suetonius (69–126) wrote, "As the Jews were making constant disturbances at the instigation of Chrestus, he [the Emperor] expelled them from Rome." The first-century Roman historians Thallus and Phlegon speak in a way that suggests that the existence of Jesus was never historically in doubt. However, from the Roman perspective, what Jesus said and did was, it seems, rather insignificant. Tacitus (56–120), one of the foremost Roman historians and a Senator, commented, "Under Tiberius [the Emperor during the public life of Jesus] nothing happened."[1]

In addition to secular histories, there are numerous extrabiblical religious sources, both Apocrypha and pseudepigrapha, that reference the person of Jesus Christ as a historical figure.[2]

Some of the more prominent extrabiblical texts provide ample evidence to the existence of Jesus. Living about two generations after St. Paul, St. Ignatius of Antioch wrote seven letters, similar in style to those of the Apostle to the Gentiles, and addressed to some of the same Christian communities, such as the Romans. These letters are filled with references to the person of Jesus. St. Clement, one of the first-century popes, also references Jesus in his letter to the Corinthians. The *Didache*, also known as *The Teaching of the Twelve Apostles*, a late second-century document, begins, "The teaching of the Lord to the Gentiles (or Nations) by the twelve apostles." "The Gospel of Thomas" describes many of the same teachings and miracles of Jesus as those narrated by the four canonical Gospel writers. "The Gospel of the Infancy of Jesus" describes many of the childhood actions of the Lord.

In chapter 3, an overview of the contents of the Gospels was provided, but a brief review can be helpful. First, it is essential to understand that the Gospels are documents of faith, written by people of faith, for people of faith; they were never intended to be biographies of Jesus. Rather, because they are documents written to particular communities at different times, they communicate the truth of Jesus using varied sources. Thus, numerous inconsistencies and conflicts, both within the Synoptic tradition and between the Synoptics and the Gospel of John, can be explained. Despite the inconsistencies, it is obvious that these documents speak of the historical significance of Jesus. What can we know precisely about Jesus from these scriptural accounts? First, we know that he was born, and that he died by crucifixion. "Second, we also know that he ran into significant conflict because of his opposition to the Jewish ruling elite, a fact that ultimately led to his death. Third, it is clear that he centered his work and mission for the estranged and marginalized of society. While Jesus reached out to all, it is clear that he had a preferential option for the poor and those that Hebrew society had forgotten. Lastly, we can say that he drew people to himself, almost like a magnet, through his miraculous cures and his teaching, which the Gospels describe as, "having authority, and not as their scribes" (Matt 7:29).

While the biblical and extrabiblical records are indeed extensive and accepted as the primary evidence to the historical reality of Jesus, especially his work and message, what can be said about the reliability of these records? Several tests can be applied to answer this question. We can first apply what is known as the bibliographic test. As addressed above, there are numerous sources that speak of the events of Jesus's life, not simply the four canonical Gospels. This abundance of resources, while noting some inconsistencies and differences in details, essentially presents a consistent picture of the events of Jesus's life and his message. Since these texts were written over a period of time, and present a coherent and consistent message, logic suggests that what these texts say is historically accurate. A second test for reliability would be to examine the authors themselves. History and Church tradition suggest that three of the four canonical evangelists (excluding John) were martyrs; the same fate was also the lot of many authors of the extrabiblical texts. One might ask why people willing to die for their faith would invent stories such as miraculous healings and the resurrection, events that might be challenged by nonbelievers. Only an author who was willing to suffer would dare to present stories that would seem outrageous to many; those who wished to save their lives would present more "acceptable" stories concerning Jesus. In a related sense, why would the writers contrive a story about a messianic figure who did not fit the classic mold (expressed powerfully in Jer 23:5–6 and Mic 5:2–5) of one who would be a powerful ruler and restore the greatness of Israel as experienced during the reigns of David and Solomon? The story of Jesus as articulated in the canonical texts, Apocrypha, and pseudepigrapha describe a messianic figure who is unacceptable to the Jews, precisely because he does not fit the mold of a great champion.

Again, playing it safe, the authors of these texts would not have claimed that Jesus was indeed the long-expected Messiah.

Additional tests to verify the veracity of the sacred texts that speak of Jesus are available. First, we can examine the test of historical geography. A few examples can be illustrative. Matthew 2:13–23 tells the story of the Holy Family's flight to Egypt to escape the clutches of King Herod. There is abundant historical evidence that many Jews during the time of Jesus actually lived outside Palestine, many near Alexandria, Egypt. Thus, the escape narrated by Matthew is very plausible. Second, historic and archaeological evidence shows that, during the time of Jesus, Nazareth was an obscure village, a fact consistent with its description in the written texts. Lastly, the Gospel evangelists mention numerous specific locations in their narratives, all of which were not only existent, but frequented by many; they were places that people of Jesus's time knew. Thus, it is clear that the evangelists were familiar with the geographic region about which they wrote.

The archaeological test is a second nonwritten method to verify the veracity of these texts and what they say about Jesus. The discovery of the "Dead Sea Scrolls" in 1948, while containing nothing about the New Testament, had numerous fragments that are consistent with the Hebrew Bible. Thus, consistency in one part of the Bible gives at least some credence to consistency in its other major division. In 1961, at Caesarea by the Sea, archaeologists discovered engraved stones that verify the rule of Pontius Pilate during the life of Jesus. Aligned with the above comment, excavations have provided evidence to the existence of the village of Nazareth during the first century of the Common Era. Lastly, archaeologists wonder why Jesus's tomb was not a place of pilgrimage as with many of the earlier prophets. One logical conclusion would be that his body was not in the tomb, providing evidence to the resurrection.

QUEST FOR THE HISTORICAL JESUS

As described earlier, the emerging paradigm of Marcus Borg, centering on the Jesus of history, is a product of the Enlightenment. Philosophers such as Voltaire, John Locke, Jean-Jacques Rousseau, and Immanuel Kant ushered in an intellectual revolution that demanded evidence for belief, challenging the basic faith upon which the earlier paradigm of the Jesus of faith was based. Thus, it was no surprise that what we know as the "quest for the historical Jesus" began to appear during this same historical era. The "first quest" centered on the idea that the Jesus of history, Borg's emerging paradigm, based on evidence, was of absolute importance for one to accept the Jesus of faith model. This "first quest" began with a German Deist, Hermann Reimarius, who claimed that the Church was a fraud from the outset; one could know nothing of the historical Jesus. In 1835, another German philosopher, David Friedrich Strauss, published a two-volume work that discounted the historical accuracy of anything in the Gospels that involved supernatural power, the direct intervention of God, or miraculous feats of Jesus. Strauss considered the Gospels to be mythic narratives.

What scholars called the "second quest" for the historical Jesus came to prominence in the late nineteenth and early twentieth centuries. Unlike the "first quest," this group of theologians saw no direct connection between the Christ of history and the Jesus of faith. One could believe through faith without verifiable historical evidence. The German theologian Martin Kahler (1835–1912) assumed the Gospels were never intended as history, certainly not as understood in a post-Enlightenment intellectual environment. He suggested that the Church was interested in presenting Jesus in a way that would make him significant in the lives of people of faith. Kahler reduced the Gospels to a series of passion narratives with extended introductions. What was truly important for him was Jesus's salvific death. The various events of his life, including the many miracles he performed, were not historically significant. Thus, as suggested above, he did not see a necessary connection between the Christ of history and the Jesus of faith. One of the twentieth century's most renowned personalities, Dr. Albert Schweitzer, who came to his greatest prominence by winning the 1952 Nobel Peace Prize for his work as a medical missionary in Africa, actually began his career as a concert pianist and later became a theologian. In 1910, he published a famous book, *Quest for the Historical Jesus*, that in essence said that there was no way to verify what the Scriptures said about Jesus in a historical sense. For example, Schweitzer wrote in his conclusion:

> The Jesus of Nazareth who came forward publicly as the Messiah, who preached the ethic of the Kingdom of God, who founded the Kingdom of Heaven upon earth, and died to give His work its final consecration, never had any existence. He is a figure designed by rationalism, endowed with life by liberalism, and clothed by modern theology in an historical garb.[3]

The contemporary quest for the historical Jesus began in the wake of the Second World War. Ernst Kasemann, a Lutheran theologian and New Testament scholar, believed that the historical Jesus was theologically indispensable; proof of the historical reality of the events of Jesus's life were absolutely critical to the Christian faith. Thus, he made a renewed call to learn more about what could be historically proven regarding the life and mission of Jesus, even in spite of the difficulties associated with such a quest. He suggested that it was important to look at history not as a series of absolute facts, but rather as events that were significant for people. This allowed him to understand the Gospel narratives in a much broader, less directly historical, and thus verifiable way. He sought to use the theological method of redaction to strip away the layers that history had placed on the events of Jesus's life, and thereby find the original core of what he said and did.[4]

The final chapter in the "quest for the historical Jesus" is found in the work of the Jesus Seminar. Beginning in 1985, a group of some 150 biblical scholars, under the direction of the American biblical scholar Robert Funk, began the process to read through the Gospels with a critical eye, asking whether the words of Jesus as recorded by the canonical evangelists were, in the minds of the scholars, actually uttered by Christ. Using available scholarship and techniques, this group produced a volume, *The Five Gospels* (1993), which was the collective effort of the scholars to analyze the four canonical Gospels and the pseudepigraphic (Gnostic) Gospel of Thomas, printing the words of Jesus in different colors in the text, depending on how certain the Seminar participants were on the accuracy of Jesus's words. These scholars placed Christ's words in three categories: those he definitely said, those he might have said, and those he most probably did not say. The Seminar stopped meeting in 2006 when Funk died. Its work marks the most recent effort in the overall scheme to investigate the historical Jesus.

CONCLUSION

While not an idea that would be prominent in the minds of most faithful Christians, the concept of the historical Jesus has significant merit. Our twenty-first-century, post-Enlightenment intellectual society seeks evidence and a rationale for most everything. It is clear that there is ample evidence, from both canonical and extrabiblical sources, as well as nonverbal tests, that Jesus not only existed, but accomplished wonderful things during his earthly life. While the narratives of the New Testament have inconsistencies and present differences in detail, they, as Vatican II clearly articulates, do present the true life of Jesus. Additionally, while the Gospel evangelists might not have direct quotes from the lips of Jesus, they certainly accurately transmitted his message. In other words, if the events narrated in the Scriptures about Jesus never happened, upon what is Christian faith based? Our investigation into the historical Jesus has, it is hoped, provided more input so we can better answer Jesus's great question to Peter: "Who do you say that I am?"

Discussion Questions

1. Do you find this analysis of the historical Jesus to be a great challenge or more of an aide to your personal faith?
2. Which of the various tests associated with validating the historical reality of Jesus is most convincing to you? Which is of least importance?
3. What is your overall opinion of the basic process described as the "quest for the historical Jesus?"
4. Many people worldwide would say that Jesus was one of the most significant people, if not the most significant person, to ever walk the earth. Why then do you think the historical record about him is so limited?
5. How significant for you is the historical reality of the various actions and words of Jesus? Is a historically verifiable Jesus as described in the Scriptures essential or tangential to your life of faith?

Chapter 6

JESUS, THE ONE WHO PRAYS

In writing to the Christian community at Colossae (Col 4:2), St. Paul proclaimed, "Devote yourselves to prayer." While a faithful and zealous Jew, Paul most assuredly was prompted to provide this important instruction through his association with Jesus. When people answer Jesus's question, "Who do you say that I am?" the idea that he was a man of prayer might be low on the list. It is not that we do not think Jesus failed to pray, but rather that, as the Son of God, he did not need to pray. When we pray we do so for several reasons. We pray for special needs, hopes, and desires; we pray in thanksgiving for the blessings we have received. We also pray in praise of God. We know that Jesus was totally divine, but he was also totally human, and the reasons we pray would be the same that Jesus spoke to his Father during his earthly life. The Scriptures provide numerous examples of Jesus asking his Father for his own needs and those of others. The Lord also prayed in thanksgiving and in praise of his Father. We will see that Jesus was actually the best and most prolific "pray-er" in Christian history. He prayed often and he prayed everywhere; he never missed an opportunity to be in communication with his Father. Thus, Jesus serves as the perfect example of a man of prayer. His fidelity to prayer and the prayers that he proclaimed can help us to answer Jesus's question, the inquiry of this book: "Who do you say that I am?"

JESUS AND PRAYER

From a Christian perspective, Jesus is the one and only true pray-er, that is one who prays, for indeed as he prays to the Father, his words are instantly heard and God responds. More importantly, it is not simply Jesus's acts of prayer, as specifically mentioned in the Gospels, but rather that his life was a prayer. We can see this clearly in that Jesus's entire earthly life was about doing the will of his Father. Indeed, that was precisely why he was sent into the world. Jesus expresses this reality quite clearly. Matthew 10:40 reads, "Whoever welcomes you welcomes me, and whoever welcomes me welcomes the one who sent me." St. John is even clearer and more specific when he reports Jesus saying, "My food is to do the will of him who sent me and to complete his work" (4:34). Jesus's prayer and the actions of his life were completely consistent. He practiced what he preached; there was no sense of hypocrisy in his life. We participate in that one prayer that Jesus addresses to his Father by asking that we be heard by the Father as Jesus was.

If we say that Jesus's whole life was a prayer, we might ask when did he specifically pray? Paul's exhortation to the Colossians quoted above was simply a challenge to do as Jesus had done during his earthly life, namely to pray always. Jesus always prayed during times of great decision in his life. After his baptism by John and before he began his public ministry, Jesus went to the desert and spent forty days and forty nights in communion with his Father. Realizing that his future ministry would be difficult and that he would be rejected by the very people to whom he was sent, the Lord gained strength for the Herculean task that lay before him. Thus, he took the time to prepare himself. We might say he went on an extended retreat, probably realizing he would never have such an opportunity in the future. St. Luke tells us that before he made the important decision of choosing his twelve apostles, the inner circle who would walk the road with him and be his initial witnesses to the world, he went to the mountain to pray (6:12–16). While Jesus certainly knew his role and the ultimate reason for his ministry, namely that he would suffer and die to atone for human sin, nevertheless before making the decision to endure his passion and death, he went to the Garden of Gethsemane and prayed earnestly to his Father. As one who was totally human, yet with divine insight, and thus knowing his future fate, he called out, "My Father, if it is possible, let this cup pass from me; yet not what I want but what you want" (Matt 26:39). The Gospel evangelists often report that Jesus retired to deserted places (e.g., Luke 5:16 and Matt 14:13) to pray. In short, Jesus's life was indeed a prayer and it was manifested by his regular and sincere conversations with his Father.

Knowing that Jesus prayed always, we could easily conclude that Jesus had no favorite place to pray. While he was certainly found praying in the synagogue of his hometown of Nazareth and his adopted city of Capernaum, there was no place that was "off-limits" to Jesus. On the contrary, Jesus was in an open field preaching to the crowd before he multiplied the loaves and fishes. As he did so St. Mark tells us that he "looked up to heaven, and blessed and broke the loaves, and gave them to his disciples to set before the people" (Mark 6:41). When, as mentioned earlier, Jesus prepared himself for his public ministry, he went to the desert. He was equally comfortable going to the mountain to pray (Matt 14:23, Mark 6:46, Luke 6:12). One of the greatest manifestations of Jesus's prayer was when he took Peter, James, and John up on a high mountain (tradition tells us Mount Tabor) and was transfigured before them. His physical transformation and the Father's words, "This is my Son, the Beloved; with him I am well pleased; listen to him!" (Matt 17:5) were manifestations of prayer.

Clearly Jesus prayed at all times and in all locations, but what was the content of his prayer? We might think that the God-man Jesus would pray in a different way or have words far beyond our mortal capability, but the Lord actually set the model for how we should pray, not only in having the resolve to pray always and everywhere, but with honesty, simplicity, and the basic rationales of petition, thanksgiving, and praise. Each Ash Wednesday the Gospel proclaimed is from St. Matthew, chapter 6, part of Jesus's famous Sermon on the Mount. Christ instructs us,

> And whenever you pray, do not be like the hypocrites; for they love to stand and pray in the synagogues and at the street corners, so that they may be seen by others. Truly I tell you, they have received their reward. But whenever you pray, go into your room and shut the door and pray to your Father who is in secret; and your Father who sees in secret will reward you. (Matt 6:5–6)

Jesus's words are crystal clear—there is no need to stand on ceremony or to be publicly seen or acknowledged for our prayer, but rather the private and simple prayer of the petitioner is most valued.

Jesus used prayer to petition his Father for the needs of others. Chapter 17 of John's Gospel is one long prayer of Jesus, asking that the Father take care of the people he will leave behind, both his apostles and those who will follow later. He prayed, "I ask not only on behalf of these, but also on behalf of those who will believe in me through their word" (John 17:20). Realizing that his public ministry will soon end, he petitions God for the needs of his disciples. All of the miracles reported by the four evangelists (there are thirty-seven in total) are examples of Jesus's physical action and words wherein he prays for others.

Jesus often prayed in thanksgiving to God. When Jesus multiplies the loaves and fish, we are told he gave thanks (Matt 15:36); when he instituted the Eucharist at the Last Supper, he once again gave thanks (Mark 14:23). Jesus gave thanks to his Father because his ministry to his apostles and disciples was effective. He prayed, "I thank you, Father, Lord of heaven and earth, because you have hidden these things from the wise and the intelligent and have revealed them to infants" (Luke 10:21).

Lastly, Jesus gave praise to God. His preaching, miracles, and even at times harsh words and challenges to the religious elite of his day were ways in which Christ gave praise to God. Christ realized that he did not act alone, but rather in response to his Father who had sent him into the world. Praying for his disciples before his passion and death, Jesus gave glory to God: "Father, the hour has come; glorify your Son so that the Son may glorify you, since you have given him authority over all people" (John 17:1–2).

It has been shown that Jesus prayed always and everywhere, and as the fully human, yet divine Son of God, raised his prayers to his Father in thanksgiving and praise as well as petition for the needs of others. Still, one might ask if Jesus ever spoke about the impact and efficacy of prayer. The answer is clearly yes! St. Luke (18:1–8) presents Jesus's parable of the persistent widow. We are told that Jesus tells the story to encourage his followers to pray always and not to lose heart. The widow's persistent pleas lead the corrupt judge to rule in her favor against her opponent. Jesus concludes the parable by telling his listeners, "And will not God grant justice to his chosen ones who cry to him day and night? Will he delay long in helping them? I tell you, he will quickly grant justice to them" (Luke 18:7–8). Even more directly, in his Sermon on the Mount, Jesus very clearly tells us that not only does God hear our prayers, but responds with what we need:

> Ask, and it will be given you; search, and you will find; knock, and the door will be opened for you. For everyone who asks receives, and everyone who searches finds, and for everyone who knocks, the door will be opened. (Matt 7:7–8)

We should note that Jesus does not say we *might* receive, that we *might* find, and the door *might* be opened. On the contrary, the Lord very clearly says these things will be provided. That's the best guarantee you will ever find because it comes from the mouth of God. In short, Jesus promises us that sincere prayer will be heard. God will grant us all that we need. However, we must be aware that what we need and what we want are not necessarily the same things.

Prayer does not remove the challenges and difficulties of life, but it does enable us to better face these situations and even to grow from them. The reward a person receives from prayer comes not in the act itself, but rather in the change it brings about in us. There is no need to impress God by our use of correct formulae. Again, we must remember Jesus's challenging words in the Sermon on the Mount, when he told the crowd, "When you are praying, do not heap up empty phrases as the Gentiles do; for they think that they will be heard because of their many words" (Matt 6:7). The Lord goes on then to synthesize the essence of all prayer by teaching his followers the Lord's Prayer. Prayer challenges us to align ourselves in trust with God and to acknowledge our need for him.

Are all methods of prayer equally effective in their ability to seek petition as well as to give praise and thanksgiving to God? Jesus provides significant insight to this question. It is clear that Christ encouraged his followers to pray privately to God. The Scriptures provide many examples of Jesus praying by himself. Earlier I mentioned Jesus's words that basically direct his followers to "pray to your Father who is in secret" (Matt 6:6). While

Jesus is certainly not in any way suggesting that community prayer is of lesser value, he is giving "high marks" to those who seek God through prayer in a more private way. Jesus certainly prayed in the synagogue and with his disciples; he was the one who commissioned the apostles, "Go therefore and make disciples of all nations, baptizing them in the name of the Father and of the Son and of the Holy Spirit" (Matt 28:19). Jesus was sending his disciples out to establish communities of faith. St. Paul, who claimed the title of apostle himself, was the foremost of the first followers of Jesus to establish local Christian communities, wherein converts could gather together and pray as a group. Again, Jesus summarizes his teaching:

> Truly I tell you, if two of you agree on earth about anything you ask, it will be done for you by my Father in heaven. For where two or three are gathered in my name, I am there among them. (Matt 18:19–20)

Thus, whether one gives praise in private or in a communal setting, it is clear that God responds, not to the content, but to the act and fidelity of prayer. It's not so much what you say, but how you say it.

THE PRAYERS OF JESUS

We have established that Jesus believed in, engaged in, and proclaimed the effectiveness of prayer, both for individuals and community. Now we need to understand better the actual prayers that Jesus left us. Quite obviously such an exploration must begin with the Lord's Prayer, the basic prayer that he taught his apostles and disciples when they asked, "Lord, teach us to pray, as John taught his disciples" (Luke 11:1). Over the course of Christian history, many famous people have made comments about the importance and purpose of the Lord's Prayer. The third-century theologian Tertullian once called it "an epitome of the whole Gospel."[1] St. Thomas Aquinas wrote,

> Among all prayers the Lord's Prayer stands preeminent, for it excels in the five conditions requisite in prayer: namely humility, assurance, rectitude, order, devotion, and humility.[2]

The twentieth-century Scripture scholar Patricia Collins added, "It has such simple, direct words. It leads us to ever deeper meanings. It stands as the very essence of our faith."[3] *The Catechism of the Catholic Church* states, "The Lord's Prayer is the quintessential prayer of the Church."[4]

What are the roots and derivation of this most fundamental of Jesus's prayers? Jesus's prayer has some similarities to the first-century Jewish Kaddish, which addressed God as "Our Father." This hymn of praise to God is generally associated with funerals, and thus is referred to as "The Mourner's Kaddish." The opening words of the prayer, "May his great name be exalted and sanctified," are drawn from Ezekiel 38:23.

For centuries Christians have memorized the Lord's Prayer, or Our Father, in the format presented by St. Matthew (6:9–13), but there are actually three different versions of this famous prayer. One form is found in the *Didache* ("The Teaching of the Twelve Apostles"), the early Christian text. St. Luke (11:2–4) has a more abbreviated form than what is commonly memorized. Luke's prayer is fully contained in Matthew's version and, in a funny twist, is considered by the biblical scholars to be the most original.[5] Matthew's version adds the petition, "Thy will be done as it is in heaven"; it also adds to the last petition the words, "and lead us not into temptation but deliver us from evil." This information begs an important question, "If Luke's version is the original, why have Christians for centuries memorized the form in Matthew's Gospel? There is a reasonable answer: Matthew's version was the one that was incorporated into the Roman Mass, giving it special status.

Analyzing the contents of the Lord's Prayer provides interesting insight for an inquiring Christian mind. Matthew's use of the Aramaic word *Abba* (basically translated, as we previously noted, as "daddy") for Father, is an invitation to the apostles to be more intimate with God, as is Jesus. Famous Scripture scholar Joachim Jeremias provides an interesting insight to Jesus's use of *Abba*: "He [Jesus] empowers them [the apostles] to speak to their Heavenly Father literally as a small child speaks to his father, in the same competent and childlike manner."[6] The Lord's Prayer then presents three specific petitions in praise of God. "Hallowed be your name," expresses the idea that God indeed must be honored. The petition "Thy kingdom come," emphasizes that we must look forward to the second coming and the establishment of God's kingdom on earth. Lastly, "Thy will be done," stresses the idea that we must be content and accept God's will in our life.

These three petitions in praise of God are followed by three more personal requests. We first ask that God provide us with our daily bread. Most scholars suggest that this is a reference to the coming of God's kingdom at the end of time, but others see it as a reference to the Eucharist. More contemporary commentators view this as a challenge for Christians to feed the hungry. We next ask God to "forgive us our debts (trespasses)." Sin is understood to be a debt to God, something we owe him, but one that cannot be repaid by human action. Jesus assures us, however, that God's forgiveness is unconditional, that it precedes our forgiveness of our fellow human beings, and that it is the basic purpose of prayer. Lastly we ask, "Lead us not into temptation (but deliver us from evil)." Why, we might ask, do we need to make such a petition—would God tempt us? Certainly, the Lord would do no such thing, but it seems to have been understood, from the earliest Judeo-Christian tradition, that people could be led into temptation unless they asked to be relieved from it. Again, some contemporary commentators suggest that this is not fear of everyday temptation, but rather that people must be protected from the final trial before death.

Clearly the Lord's Prayer is the most basic and famous of all Jesus's prayers in the New Testament, but there are others that are highly significant. The aforementioned "Priestly Prayer" of John's chapter 17 is certainly worth some analysis. In this prayer Jesus prays for himself, but for his disciples as well. He realizes his hour has come; the end of his mission, his public ministry, is just around the corner. He clearly emphasizes the importance of his teaching, stating, "For the words that you gave to me I have given to them, and they have received them" (John 17:8). This is clearly a prayer of unity. He wants his band of followers to be one with each other: "I ask…that they may all be one. As you, Father, are in me and I am in you, may they also be in us, so that the world may believe that you have sent me" (John 17:20–21).

Jesus's prayer in the Garden of Gethsemane says many things about him and also provides significant challenges to his followers. Initially Jesus tells his apostles, "Sit here while I go over there and pray" (Matt 26:36). His prayer presents a fourfold invitation: to stillness—stillness of the heart, to trust—we must choose to trust, to be humble, to seek self-knowledge. The full humanity of Jesus is on display when he prays, "My Father, if it is possible, let this cup pass from me; yet not what I want but what you want" (Matt 26:39). From a human perspective, yet knowing his future, he asks to be relieved from his fate. In the end, however, he places God's will above his own; his acceptance is total.

The famous "Seven Last Words" that Christ spoke from the cross will close out our investigation of Jesus as the great pray-er. Collectively seen, these seven prayers demonstrate his humanity, compassion for others, and acceptance of his role as the one sent into the world to redeem mankind. Thinking of others before himself, Jesus reaches out, to both friend and foe. He holds no animosity toward those responsible for his death: "Father, forgive them; for they do not know what they are doing" (Luke 23:34). Concerned about those who will be left behind, he calls out to his mother and the Beloved Disciple: "'Woman, here is your son'....'Here is your mother'" (John 19:26–27). He even reaches out to the "good thief" who, realizing that Jesus has been unjustly punished, asks for his assistance. Jesus replies, "Today you will be with me in Paradise" (Luke 23:43). From the human perspective, Jesus's physical need prompts him to say, "I am thirsty" (John 19:28). From a similar standpoint, Jesus calls upon his Father: "My God, my God, why have you forsaken me? (Matt 27:46; Mark 15:34). In the end, however, Jesus accepts his fate. Realizing that the end is near and most probably with a diminished voice, Jesus says, "It is finished" (John 19:30). In the final submission of his will to that of the Father, he breathes his last and prays, "Father, into your hands, I commend my spirit" (Luke 23:46). These seven prayers, the last recorded of Jesus in the Gospels prior to his resurrection, encapsulate the entirety of his life—his humanity, outreach, and compassion for others, yet always with obedience to the will of his Father.

CONCLUSION

Our basic inquiry, asking "Who do you say that I am?" has been given some important input by an analysis of Jesus as the great pray-er and the prayers he proclaimed, as recorded in the Gospels. Do you relate to Jesus as a man of prayer, one who by word and action was himself a pray-er and challenged his followers to fall in line with his example? Certainly, the example that Jesus set in praying always and everywhere, and the guarantee he provided that our prayer would always be heard and we would receive what we need, must certainly have some bearing on how we answer the basic question of this book. In imitation of Jesus and millions who have come after him, contemporary Christians must answer the call and take up the challenge to be men and women of prayer. How, when, where, and even why we pray are not, as our investigation has shown, truly relevant questions. Rather, the great responsibility is to refuse to make excuses for our failure to pray. All followers of Jesus must respond to this challenge.

Discussion Questions

1. In your opinion, what is the greatest challenge that Jesus as the ultimate pray-er presents to individual Christians and the Christian community collectively?
2. Which aspect of prayer do you find most challenging in your life? What can Jesus's life of prayer teach you about your own personal prayer life?
3. Which of the prayers of Jesus found in the Scriptures is most attractive to you? Which is the most challenging? Why?
4. Do we truly believe that God not only hears, but also responds to our prayer in ways that are best for us? Do we become frustrated when we perceive that "God is not listening" or that "God has not answered my prayers?"
5. As we have seen, prayer does not change God, but it can and must change us in ways that will allow us to accept God's will in our life. What experiences of prayer in your life have you found transformative—times when you could truly see that God was molding you to accept certain realities or possibly to prepare you for a future reality?

Chapter 7

JESUS, THE REVERSER OF ROLES

The Gospel narratives and historical research have concluded that in approximately 30 CE, Jesus of Nazareth was executed as a common criminal on a hill called Golgotha, just outside Jerusalem. But why did Jesus receive capital punishment? Was it for his religious views? Was it for his political views? Was his social perspective unacceptable? Again, while people claimed that Jesus was the Messiah, he did not fit the mold of the prophecy found in Jeremiah (23:5–6) or Micah (5:2–5). He was not a warrior; he did not seek political freedom for Israel. Many people proclaimed that he was a king. In fact, the inscription on his cross read, "This is Jesus, King of the Jews." Still others suggested that Jesus was the Son of God. One thing that is clear about Jesus was that he was a radical in every way, as we would so define a person today. He challenged the establishment; he refused to accept authority as it was found in the Jewish religious elite. He rejected absolute adherence to the law, Jewish tradition, and custom. He ridiculed the purity system that separated individuals and groups from one another. He freely associated with "undesirable" peoples of all ranks: lepers, foreigners, women, prostitutes, and tax collectors. Jesus broke every convention in the book—political, social, and religious.

Why was Jesus of Nazareth executed as a common criminal? In short, his behavior and teachings turned the world upside down. Jesus transformed people's thinking; he provided an alternative to conventional wisdom. Jesus was not a criminal, nor a rogue, but his challenge to the prevailing system and those who oversaw it was simply too much. Jesus Christ was put to death because he reversed the roles. Such a reversal in thinking could not be tolerated.

JESUS AND THE POLITICS OF COMPASSION

Jesus, a practicing Jewish man, was born into a society that was dominated by the concept of holiness. Leviticus 19:2 reads, "You shall be holy, for I the LORD your God am holy." This concept of holiness was rooted in the basics of the law, given to Moses by God on Mount Sinai (Exod 20:1–19). The law and its strict application in every aspect of life was a central tenet of Jewish society; any suggestion that the law did not have full authority in virtually all situations was intolerable to the practicing Jew, especially the religious elite.

Jesus, however, offered an alternative to the concept of holiness and the centrality of the law. Jesus suggested that mercy (compassion) was of greater significance. He proclaimed, "Be merciful, just as your Father is merciful" (Luke 6:36). Jesus did not come to destroy Jewish tradition, but rather to bring an aspect of God's love and compassion that was missing. Again he proclaimed, "I have come not to abolish [the law] but to fulfill" (Matt 5:17).

Jesus's new approach was manifested most especially in how he questioned the purpose of the Sabbath and challenged the established purity system of Jewish society. He questioned whether it was more important to eat than to obey the Sabbath proscriptions against the gathering of food (Matt 12:1–8; Mark 2:23–28; Luke 6:1–5); he asked whether it was possible to cure someone of disease or illness on the Sabbath (Matt 12:10; Luke 14:3). He summarized his teaching by saying, "The sabbath was made for humankind, and not humankind for the sabbath; so the Son of Man is lord even of the sabbath" (Mark 2:27–28).

The purity system, as central as the Sabbath to Jewish life, had become a political and social system as well. For Jews, a hierarchy of purity, based to some extent on birth, created polarities of pure versus impure, clean versus unclean. Jews were clean; Gentiles were unclean. The temple and its priests stood at the apex of the purity ranks. However, the system was in direct conflict with the politics of compassion that Jesus preached. One might say that when Jesus substituted compassion for holiness, he indicted the holiness system.

The New Testament provides many examples of how Jesus attacked the purity system of his day, substituting his concept of compassion. In a preferential way, Jesus reached out to people who were considered impure. He touched lepers (Matt 8:1–4) and allowed a hemorrhaging woman to touch him (Mark 5:25–34). He cast demons out of foreigners (Mark 5:1–20) and held significant conversations with women (John 4:7–42). He dined with tax collectors (Mark 2:13–17) and was associated with prostitutes (Matt 21:31–32; John 8:2–11). He was inclusive in all his personal relationships, holding open table fellowship with anyone who was willing to listen. Jesus presented a fellowship of equals. Perhaps the best example is the famous parable of the Good Samaritan (Luke 10:25–37). In the story Jesus speaks of a traveler who falls among robbers, is beaten severely, and left to die. A priest and a Levite, both upstanding members of the Jewish religious elite, have the opportunity, one after the other, to assist the man. A twenty-first century reader is appalled that these two men simply pass by, offering no assistance. A reader contemporaneous with Jesus, however, would have understood that for the priest or Levite to touch the man would have rendered him impure and thus unable to perform his religious duties until he completed ritual purification. When Jesus then makes a passing Samaritan, an ancestor of the lost kingdom of Israel and the most dreaded and hated of peoples during Jesus's day, the hero who assists the injured man, the indictment of the purity system is made very clear. Jesus is making a statement: compassion is more important than strict adherence to the law and its system of purity. For Jesus, where purity divides and excludes, compassion unites and includes.

THE EXECUTION OF JESUS: WHY?

One of the few events that all four Gospel evangelists describe, and certainly the story that is given the greatest detail, is Jesus's crucifixion. Many biblical scholars suggest the crucifixion narrative was the first part of each Gospel written, with various details of Jesus's ministry being described as a prelude to this detailed story of Jesus's passion and death. On the Friday prior to the Jewish celebration of Passover, in approximately the year 30 CE, Jesus of Nazareth was executed by order of Roman authorities at Golgotha, a lonely hill outside the holy city of Jerusalem. Crucifixion was a form of capital punishment common in the Roman world, but a form of execution that was generally reserved for serious crimes. From our knowledge of Jesus through a personal reading of the Gospels, as well as the multiple images that have been presented in this volume, there does not appear to be any words or actions from Jesus that would warrant his being publicly executed as a common criminal. It seems, therefore, in our investigation that we must ask why Jesus was executed. Why was a man who cured people of various afflictions, promoted peace and love, prayed to God for others, and preached a message of compassion be "rewarded" by being put to death? How can this central and tragic event in the life of Jesus help us to answer the question of our investigation, "Who do you say that I am?"

Various reasons for the death of Jesus have historically been put forward. Was he executed due to his religious views, his political stance, or his social justice platform? Many Jews saw him as a rabbi and, therefore, a religious leader. Yet he often criticized the Jewish religious authorities, especially the Pharisees. He was rather apolitical, claiming, "Give therefore to the emperor the things that are the emperor's, and to God the things that are God's" (Matt 22:21). He spoke out on behalf of foreigners, the diseased, and others who stood on the margins of Hebrew society; he was in some ways a social activist. But do such ideas constitute grounds for execution? Jesus was heralded by some to be the long-anticipated Messiah; he indirectly claimed to be King of the Jews. Indeed, the sign placed above his head on the cross read in Hebrew, Latin, and Greek, "Jesus—King of the Jews." But Jesus did not fit the mold of the Messiah as was prophesied by Jeremiah (23:5–6) or Micah (5:2–6). The former told the Hebrews in Judah,

> The days are surely coming, says the LORD, when I will raise up for David a righteous Branch, and he shall reign as king and deal wisely, and shall execute justice and righteousness in the land. In his days Judah will be saved and Israel will live in safety.

Jesus may have claimed to be King, but the Roman occupation continued. Judah remained captive; Israel was in disarray.

How could Jesus claim to be the Messiah and none of Jeremiah's prophecy be fulfilled? Some of his disciples saw Jesus as the Son of God. Indeed, he was so proclaimed when he calmed the storm (Mark 4:35–41) and walked on the sea (Matt 14:22–33). Such words and actions were blasphemous, as Judaism was the first monotheistic religion. Thus, the question remains, what were the reasons behind the execution of Jesus?

JESUS: A TRUE RADICAL

Clearly, Jesus was a radical in every way, as we would define such a person in our contemporary society. Not only did he claim, and others assert for him, special titles, but more importantly he challenged the establishment and the religious elite of his time. He constantly challenged and even ridiculed the Jewish religious elite, especially the Pharisees, for their self-righteousness and scorn of others. He challenged the law, which from the time of Moses was central to Jewish self-understanding. Indeed, Jesus often placed people and their needs above the dictates of the law. Jesus associated freely with groups and individuals, whether they were women, immigrants, or the sick, who were considered undesirable. Jesus broke through every convention of Jewish society. He was like the prophets of the Old Testament, who took on the authorities of their day and spoke out for the marginalized. He was an advocate of social justice. Indeed, Jesus of Nazareth was executed as a common criminal because he did not fit into Hebrew society. He turned the Jewish world upside down so severely that his presence, as far as the Jewish ruling elite was concerned, could no longer be tolerated. In essence, Jesus Christ was executed because he was a radical who did not fit the mold others had made for him.

JESUS: TEACHER OF ALTERNATIVE WISDOM

The aforementioned politics of compassion that Jesus highlighted in his ministry created significant conflict with the Jewish religious elite, and certainly became a major rationale for his death. Jesus reversed the norms of society and developed a new form of wisdom than that traditionally understood in Judaism. The conventional wisdom of Jesus's day was, like any general understanding of his life, shaped in large part by culture and tradition. Conventional wisdom provided guidance on how one was to live; it embodied the central values of the culture. Such wisdom was based on a system of rewards and punishments; you reap what you sow. Conventional wisdom had both social and psychological consequences. Socially, it created a world of hierarchies; psychologically, it became the basis for identity and self-esteem. Such wisdom, in the mind of Jesus, forced people to live a life of bondage to a dominant culture. People were measured by how they compared to a standard. This philosophy was not exclusive to first-century Israel; on the contrary, the religious scholar Marcus Borg, in his book *Meeting Jesus Again for the First Time*, suggests that such conventional wisdom was not only the norm; it was pervasive. Jesus saw such a philosophy as a life of requirements.

In contrast to the conventional wisdom, Jesus offered an alternative. The New Testament presents Jesus as the embodiment, the reincarnation of a divine wisdom. Using aphorisms and parables, Jesus guided his followers to see what others might not see, a way of viewing God that contrasted with conventional wisdom. While many aphorisms, such as "You cannot serve two masters" or "Let the dead bury the dead," are strung together, as seen in the Sermon on the Mount, they most likely were originally uttered numerous times but in a single phrase. Similarly, the parables of Jesus, presented by the Gospel evangelists in varied literary forms, were used to deconstruct the conventional wisdom of his day, a wisdom that turned societal norms on their head. Jesus used the language of paradox and reversal to present an alternative wisdom. For example, what is happening when a Samaritan is seen as the hero and a priest and a Levite are viewed as callous villains (Luke 10:25–37)? What type of world suggests that those who are poor, those who mourn, or those who are persecuted for their faith are blessed (Matt 5:1–12)? How is it possible that the last will be first and the first will be last (Matt 20:16)? There seems to be something radically wrong when Jesus proclaims, "All who exalt themselves will be humbled, and all who humble themselves will be exalted" (Matt 23:12). Why would Jesus say that the narrow, less traveled, and more difficult path, as opposed to the wide and easier way, is the only path to life (Matt 7:13–14)? Those who follow the scrutiny of conventional wisdom found little merit in Jesus's words; rather, his teaching, which reversed the norms of Hebrew society, was seen as a threat.

Jesus gave a new image to God. Rather than viewing God as the judge or one who mandated requirements to be met, the view of conventional wisdom, Jesus offered an image of God as gracious and compassionate. In the parable of the prodigal son, the image of the father with his arms outstretched waiting on the hill for his young son to return is the image Jesus proposes for God. Although the wayward young man has prepared a speech for his father, not one word is uttered before the elder man's compassion is manifested by clothing his son in finery, killing the fatted calf, and hosting a celebration. The narrow path of Jesus's unconventional wisdom invites us to see God as gracious rather than as an enforcer of requirements and boundaries. Additionally, there is an invitation to a life centered in God. The alternative wisdom of Jesus sees daily life as a deepening of one's person; the spirit of God is not a life of requirements and reward. Jesus called his followers to an internal transformation, centering their life on God, not on any external law. As he overturned the tables of the money changers in the temple in a fit of righteous anger (John 2:13–22), so too did Jesus upset traditional thinking concerning one's relationship with God.

JESUS BRINGS A NEW TORAH

The alternative wisdom that Jesus proposed, which was viewed as such a significant threat by the Jewish religious elite, was in essence a rewriting of the Torah. The straightforward, detailed, and very precise stipulations presented in the Pentateuch, totaling 613 specific laws to be followed, were replaced by a roadmap for the Church, a model of faith. The heart of Jesus's teaching is found in the Sermon on the Mount (Matt 5—7), which begins with the powerful words of the Beatitudes. Here Jesus uses a series of paradoxes that turn standards of the world upside down. Throughout his teaching Jesus suggests that the last will be first and the first will be last; he exalts those who have the courage to hold themselves in check and humbles those who think themselves important. Outsiders are made important, women are respected, and the poor are granted the privilege of his presence. Jesus presented a new wisdom: to walk by faith required one to be a contradiction to the world. Such thoughts were too much for many to handle.

Jesus, however, did not "throw out the baby with the bathwater"; he came not to abolish the law but to fulfill it (Matt 5:17–19). The letter of the law, as laid down so precisely in the Pentateuch, was now joined by the spirit of the law. Thus, for Jesus the new Torah was not a rejection of the past, but rather the addition of righteousness. Jesus added himself to the law. In essence, Jesus took the 365 negative and 248 positive commandments of Moses and reduced them to following him. Jesus transformed the social order from God-centered legislation to freedom for humanity. In the Sermon on the Mount, the love of God and neighbor were made inseparable. Jesus transferred the juridical and social ordinances from the immediate purview of the divine and made them the responsibility of enlightened reason. In this sense Jesus was not a rebel or liberal, but rather the prophetic interpreter of the Torah. Jesus does not abolish the law; he fulfills it.

Thus, we must return to the basic question: Why was Jesus of Nazareth executed as a common criminal? What had he done that warranted such punishment? First, Jesus challenged the prevailing Jewish system of order, the conventional wisdom of his day. He challenged the absoluteness of the law, offering compassion over purity. Jesus confronted the religious authorities of his day. He came to fulfill the law, to provide a second vital aspect, the spirit, to the Mosaic Law specified in the Torah. Jesus was countercultural; he was not afraid to stand against the tide. In short, Jesus reversed the norms of society, a process that appeared so threatening to the religious elite that they sought his death.

For the Jews of Jesus's day, the challenges he presented were simply unacceptable and, therefore, the decision was made to remove him from the scene. What does this say to all of us if we seek to be true disciples? To be countercultural, to stand up for what we believe, to hold fast against the prevailing tide of a world often antithetical to Christian belief is not an easy road, yet it is the path Jesus mapped out for his followers. Jesus was executed as a common criminal because he did not fit the mold of the society in which he lived. Few, if any of us, will suffer the same fate as Jesus, but if we live our Christian vocation well, suffering will come our way. Let us remember the words of Jesus as our consolation: "Blessed are you when people revile you and persecute you and utter all kinds of evil against you falsely on my account. Rejoice and be glad, for your reward is great in heaven" (Matt 5:11–12).

CONCLUSION

The basic question of our quest, "Who do you say that I am?" has now been furnished with another angle, the reality that Jesus was someone who challenged the prevailing system so significantly, reversed societal norms so greatly, that those in charge felt he had to be eliminated. From the perspective of the people of his day, Jesus was a rebel, someone who did not fit neatly into Hebrew society. In our contemporary world we often encounter people who challenge society, and because of their "unacceptable ideas," they are set aside, placed on the margins, and silenced. Is a contemporary face of Jesus found in one of these people whom society seemingly cannot absorb or tolerate? Can we find Jesus in the person whom we have cast aside in our lives? Indeed, pondering Jesus as a reverser of roles, a reality that led to his execution, forces us to answer this question, as distasteful as it might be. What we discover about ourselves in the process, however, will certainly help us to know the Lord better, to find him in others, and to eventually attain eternal life.

Discussion Questions

1. Have I, unknowingly or unwittingly, through my thoughts and/or actions brought pain and suffering to others, especially to the poor and those who stand on the margins, those who are the contemporary face of Christ?

2. Does the fact that Jesus was a true radical in his society change or alter how I view him and people who are labeled as "radicals" today?

3. Jesus's unconventional approach to life was problematic for many people of his time. Does his use of compassion help you

to understand the impact he had on people and prompt you to be equally compassionate in your life?

4. While Jesus's claims to be Messiah and King were certainly challenged by the people of his day, it seems that his overall challenge to the "system" common at that time was what tipped the scales against him. What does this say to you about Jesus and your role as his contemporary disciple?
5. Does the reality that Jesus basically died as a common criminal in any way change your image of him? As we close our investigation, how does this reality impact your answer to the Lord's question, "Who do you say that I am?"

Chapter 8

JESUS'S MISSION AND THE KINGDOM OF GOD

Our investigation of the classic question of Jesus, "Who do you say that I am?" has been directed to various images or roles that for centuries Christians have discussed and pondered. These images, as we have seen, run the spectrum of ideas; the various roles he serves are equally diverse. An important element of the conversation between Jesus and Peter, however, actually happens after Peter responds to the Lord's question, stating, "You are the Messiah, the Son of the living God" (Matt 16:16). Jesus compliments Peter for his insight and then goes on to say, "And I tell you, you are Peter, and on this rock I will build my church, and the gates of Hades will not prevail against it. I will give you the keys of the kingdom of heaven, and whatever you bind on earth will be bound in heaven, and whatever you loose on earth will be loosed in heaven" (Matt 16:18–19). Roman Catholics have always understood Jesus's words to Peter as the initiation of the Church with Peter as the appointed head or first pope.

Jesus's words to Peter speak of two related ideas, the specific mission of Christ, and the concept of the "kingdom of heaven." What specifically was the mission of Jesus? One might rightly answer that his basic mission was to redeem the world; another person might say he came to present a model for daily living. A third person, however, might suggest that the Lord's mission was to inaugurate this "kingdom of heaven," or as it is often referred to the "kingdom of God." What did Jesus mean by the kingdom of God? The answer is not as simple as one might think, for as will be explored in this chapter, there are several plausible understandings. Is the kingdom of God a political school of thought, a reality in the heart of the believer, some future kingdom that we must seek, or a present reality that we must daily build and foster? Exploring how these ideas are understood and how we might participate in them will certainly be helpful in our overall quest. Thus, when seeking to answer who Jesus is for us as individuals, his role as founder of the Church and initiator of the kingdom of God must be considered.

THE MISSION OF JESUS IN THE SYNOPTIC GOSPELS

The mission of Jesus as depicted by the Synoptic evangelists is divided into three separate time periods. First is the mission in Galilee, comprising the majority of Jesus's public life. During this period Jesus moves about in the northern regions of Israel, speaking of his mission by his preaching and acting on it through his miracles, exorcisms, and physical cures. These three evangelists, especially Mark, describe how Jesus constantly found himself in conflict with the Pharisees over his mission of compassion that at times conflicted with the Hebrew law. This conflict, of course, eventually sets up the rationale for Jesus's arrest and crucifixion. During this period as well Jesus calls his apostles, gathers others around him, and even sends them forth to do the work he initiated. The second part of Jesus's mission can be described as his movement from Galilee to Jerusalem. Recall that the Synoptic writers describe Jesus's public ministry as one year based on their consistent narrative that he went to Jerusalem only once. This section of the Synoptics also finds Jesus in conflict, but now with temple authorities. Much of his teachings about discipleship are found in this section. The last section of Jesus's mission relates to the final week of his life in Jerusalem, including his triumphal entry celebrated on Palm Sunday through the resurrection.

How do the three Synoptic evangelists speak of Jesus's mission; what was central to his actions and words? Mark almost evenly divides the Galilean ministry, the majority of his work, between Jesus as healer and teacher. Matthew and Luke, on the other hand, concentrate much more on the mission of Jesus as a teacher. In fact, teacher is a very common title for Jesus in these latter two Gospels. Jesus taught for the most part in informal settings; only rarely do we hear him preaching in the synagogue or the temple. As we have seen in an earlier chapter, Jesus used parables as his primary vehicle for teaching, for they communicated a message that was well hidden to some, was obvious to others, and, equally important, proved timeless, allowing these stories to become teachable moments even today.

An important question to ask at this stage is what precisely was Jesus's mission? Was his central mission about heaven and the afterlife, or did he center his teaching in other areas? As a great prophet, Jesus, like his many predecessors in the Old Testament, spoke about the future, but as we learned earlier, the majority of what the prophets of old described were the ongoing problems in Israel during their lifetimes. Thus, in a similar way, Jesus's mission was about the people, needs, and problems present in his then contemporary environment. All of his actions helped specific people of his time; his teaching, such as his Sermon on the Mount, basically addressed the needs of the people he encountered. But the timelessness of Scripture allows us to find great merit and contemporary understanding in both the actions and the words of Jesus from two thousand years ago. Jesus spoke and acted for his day, but his mission speaks for all people at all times.

Clearly Jesus's mission was itinerant. The Gospels narrate how Jesus was constantly on the move during his Galilean ministry. While his main "station" was Capernaum, a major center of trading during the time of Jesus and thus a place that allowed him to encounter many different people, Jesus was constantly traveling from one place to another, seeking to reach as many people as possible. He crisscrossed the Sea of Galilee numerous times, returned to his native place of Nazareth, and even traveled at times outside the confines of Israel.

Besides being itinerant, it is clear that Jesus's mission was primarily to the Jewish people, for he indeed was the promised Messiah, although he did encounter non-Jews in his ministry. All three Synoptic writers report that Jesus went north of Israel into the region of Tyre and Sidon, where he encountered a Syro-Phoenician woman whose daughter was ill (Mark 7:24–30; Matt 15:21–28). They also report that he traveled to the region of the Decapolis (southeast of the Sea of Galilee). Jesus was constantly on the move, for his mission was to encounter as many of the "lost sheep of Israel" as he could in order to show them the proper way to life.

There are numerous things that can be said in a collective way about the mission of Jesus as recorded by the Synoptic evangelists, but his conflicts with the hierarchy of Jewish society were clearly one idea at the top of Jesus's agenda. He did not seek conflict, but his words and actions were often seen as intolerable by the Jewish scholars of the law. Jesus's mission raised conflict with the religious elite of his day over such things as Sabbath practice and the purity system. Most of the religious elite who encountered Jesus were blind to his mission. Matthew reports Jesus saying, "Do not think that I have come to abolish the law or the prophets; I have come not to abolish but to fulfill" (Matt 5:17). Jesus came to fill in what was missing in the law, namely its spirit. The letter of the law was well-known and certainly carefully guarded in Jesus's day, especially by the religious elite. They could not imagine a rabbi, let alone one who claimed to be the Messiah, breaking any law; especially doing so with some regularity and with no apparent concern for the sanctity of the law from the time of Moses.

Beyond the conflict aspect of Jesus's mission, several significant ideas are prevalent in the Synoptic accounts of Jesus's ministry. First, Jesus was certainly a Jewish mystic. What he taught was not always direct and clear. This is certainly understandable with the knowledge that Jesus was divine as well as human, something that was probably lost on the majority of those who encountered him. Next, Jesus was clearly a healer and an exorcist. The Gospels are filled with accounts of physical healings of people, whether an individual directly, or a relative or even a servant of the one making the petition. Jesus used his mission to cast out demons, such as his exorcising evil spirits from a boy (Mark 9:14–29) and the many demons of Legion (Mark 5:1–20). Third, Jesus was a teacher of wisdom. He offered wisdom as the base, the spirit that needed to be added to the letter of the law to make it complete. Fourth, Jesus was a great prophet who predicted much about his own future, but more importantly pointed out the errors of society, and presented positive teachings for the betterment of all. Lastly, an integral part of Jesus's mission was to inaugurate the Church. His proclamation to Peter, calling him the rock upon which he would build his Church and presenting him with the keys necessary to bind and loose, initiated in a formal way the institution of the Church that has served the Christian people faithfully from that moment to the present day.

JESUS'S MISSION AND THE KINGDOM OF GOD

The multiple aspects of the mission of Jesus detailed above, while seemingly inclusive, lack one central idea that permeates much of Jesus's teaching. Running as a constant thread throughout the fabric of Jesus's mission and teaching is his idea of the "kingdom of God," or as he often expresses it, the "kingdom of heaven." What specifically did Jesus mean? Why does he speak of this so frequently and in varied ways through his teaching, especially in the parables? The terms "kingdom of God" and "kingdom of heaven" are found in the Synoptic Gospels in sixty-one separate places; yet, there is no precise clarity or uniformity on precisely what Jesus meant by these expressions. What is the kingdom; when will it come or has it already arrived? Is the kingdom a present reality or future hope? Does it refer to a spiritual or political expectation? Seeking a better understanding of this central idea of Jesus's mission, what he meant, and how his words have been understood can greatly assist us in our quest to understand better and answer the Lord's question to Peter: "Who do you say that I am?"

While the specific understanding of what Jesus meant by his terms "kingdom of God" and "kingdom of Heaven" is not absolutely clear, their use in his parables and teachings have been categorized under three basic scenarios. The first of these speaks of how one ends their exile from God and finds the proper path home. The parable of the sower and its explanation (Matt 13:1–9, 18–23; Mark 4:1–9, 13–20) is one example. Jesus speaks of the Word of God being trampled, stifled, and stolen, but eventually falling on good soil, a reference to an individual finally appreciating God's word and growing from it. For both evangelists Jesus uses parables to describe the kingdom. Possibly an even better example is the famous parable of the prodigal son

(Luke 15:11–32). Familiar to us all, the prodigal's self-exile ends when he realizes his need for his family.

The second generic scenario calls for the renewal of the Jewish people. Christ calls his fellow Jews to repentance and to belief. The Sermon on the Mount is probably the best example, as it is one very long exhortation for the people to be the community of faith that they were called to be by God. Jesus's images of salt and light are extremely illustrative. He says,

> You are the salt of the earth; but if salt has lost its taste, how can its saltiness be restored? It is no longer good for anything, but is thrown out and trampled under foot.
>
> You are the light of the world. A city built on a hill cannot be hid. No one after lighting a lamp puts it under the bushel basket, but on the lampstand, and it gives light to all in the house. In the same way, let your light shine before others, so that they may see your good works and give glory to your Father in heaven. (Matt 5:13–16)

In essence, Jesus was calling people to be part of the new role Israel was to fulfill in the world, whether that be to prepare the world for a future kingdom of God or to build the kingdom that had already been inaugurated by Jesus himself.

Jesus's third general teaching on the kingdom speaks of disaster and vindication that will come upon Israel unless the community of faith fulfills the mission it was given by God. Luke reports how Jesus, in a rather mournful way, looked upon the holy city of Jerusalem, lamenting its failures:

> If you, even you, had only recognized on this day the things that make for peace! But now they are hidden from your eyes. Indeed, the days will come upon you,

> when your enemies will set up ramparts around you and surround you, and hem you in on every side. They will crush you to the ground, you and your children within you, and they will not leave within you one stone upon another; because you did not recognize the time of your visitation from God. (Luke 19:46–44)

Jesus's disappointment in those who failed to recognize him and the kingdom he brought was almost tangible. His compassion for his people never wavered, even when their disloyalty and lack of fidelity could, as the evangelists proclaim, bring him to tears.

In his book *The Method and Message of Jesus' Teachings*, scripture scholar Robert Stein presents four different models that help explain what Jesus might have meant by the term "the kingdom of God." On a wholly pragmatic level, Stein offers his "political school," suggesting that the "kingdom of God" was a reference to the establishment of a political kingdom on earth. As the Messiah was sent to restore the greatness of Israel to the glory of the days of Kings David and Solomon, it makes practical sense that Jesus would want to establish some type of political reign that could be continued by his followers after his earthly life had ended. A second model is referred to as the "non-eschatological school." Here Stein is suggesting that Jesus's idea of the kingdom of God has nothing to do with the *eschaton*, or as it is commonly known, the second coming of Christ. In this model, the kingdom of heaven refers to God's special presence in the heart of all believers. Rather than a physical kingdom, this model suggests that Jesus wanted to implant in the hearts and minds of his followers a longing for one's future return to God. A third model, "the consistent eschatological school," suggests that the kingdom that Jesus sought to build will indeed be present when he returns. Stein's fourth model, "the realized eschatology school," suggests that Jesus has already built the kingdom, that it exists today, and, therefore, we have the responsibility to continue to refine its construction (*Method and Message*, 60–81).

Providing examples for Robert Stein's aforementioned models can be helpful to our overall quest, for they can help us to understand not only what the kingdom might be, but what it says about Jesus. Although used as a model in describing the kingdom of God, the concept of Jesus inaugurating a political party while on earth is not descriptive to any of the many instances in which he uses the expression. It seems that Jesus was rather apolitical in the way he approached society. Rather, his "political" aspirations would be found more in a mode of social justice, specifically his outreach to those who stood on the margins. He was their advocate, even when people stood outside due to their non-Jewish status. For example, there was the Roman centurion who asked Jesus to cure his servant (Matt 8:5–13); the Syro-Phoenician woman whose daughter was ill (Mark 7:24–30); physical illness, such as leprosy (Mark 1:40–45); occupation, such as a tax collector who was viewed as a collaborator with the Roman occupiers (Mark 2:13–17); or sinful status, such as the woman caught in adultery (John 8:2–11). Jesus's role was completely countercultural. In this sense he rejected political status, choosing, rather, to be a basic nonconformist.

Robert Stein's political school might not produce any overt examples in the Synoptic tradition, but his non-eschatological school has several examples. One is found in the Book of Mark:

> No one sews a piece of unshrunk cloth on an old cloak; otherwise, the patch pulls away from it, the new from the old, and a worse tear is made. And no one puts new wine into old wineskins; otherwise, the wine will burst the skins, and the wine is lost, and so are the skins; but one puts new wine into fresh wineskins. (2:21–22)

Here Jesus is suggesting that his kingdom requires one to be open to what is new. This interior journey requires a change of heart, what the Greeks called *metanoia*. One becomes interiorly ready for the kingdom by having the wisdom and the courage to accept that which is different, that which may require one to change or transform oneself. Using these words of Jesus as an example, the kingdom of God will be constructed person-by-person in the individual's heart.

The consistent eschatological school, suggesting that the kingdom of God will be inaugurated when Jesus comes again at the end of time, can be illustrated by Luke's twofold story of the tower and the battle (14:28–32) and Matthew's parable of the treasure, pearl, and net (13:44–48). In the first story Jesus cautions his listeners to prepare well for the forthcoming kingdom. He says a man will not begin to build a tower unless he knows he has the resources for its completion. He goes on to say that the king will not order his troops into battle against a superior force if he knows that he cannot secure victory. Thus, Jesus is asking his apostles in a similar way to prepare themselves for the kingdom that will one day come. In Matthew, Jesus suggests that the wise person will sell everything that he possesses in order to own the treasure in the field or the pearl of great price. Similarly, the dragnet thrown into the sea will not necessarily save one, but only those deemed worthy. All in all, these stories seem to describe the kingdom of God as a future reality, something that is sought but can only be found when one encounters Christ, who will reconcile the world to himself at his second coming.

The realized eschatological school, on the other hand, speaks of the kingdom of God present today. Mark 4:30–32 reports Jesus saying,

> With what can we compare the kingdom of God, or what parable will we use for it? It is like a mustard seed, which, when sown upon the ground, is the

> smallest of all the seeds on earth; yet when it is sown it grows up and becomes the greatest of all shrubs, and puts forth large branches, so that the birds of the air can make nests in its shade.

Many interpret Jesus's words to mean that he has planted the seed of the kingdom but it has not reached its full maturity. It is the work of his followers to do what they can to make the kingdom what it was intended to be. St. Luke's parable of the great supper (14:15–24) describes a great dinner that has been prepared, but the invited guests refuse to come. Understanding the dinner to be the kingdom that has been inaugurated with Jesus's public ministry, it is easy to see why the Lord was so critical of the people to whom he was sent, those who rejected his message and mission. Thus, the banquet, an image for the kingdom, will be offered to those who are not initially invited, namely to the Gentiles. The kingdom of God has arrived, but it is our responsibility to recognize and accept it.

CONCLUSION

Jesus was sent into the world by his Father to inaugurate a mission. His miracles, message, and especially his proclamation of the kingdom of God, attracted many, but simultaneously generated fear and much consternation in the minds of those who were challenged by his actions and words. He became a marked man in Hebrew society for the way he challenged both the system and those who were intricately involved with it. Many would suggest, however, that his primary purpose was to inaugurate the kingdom of God, an idea that Jesus expressed often, but without sufficient clarity to know precisely what he meant. Was Jesus speaking about some political aspect of his ministry or was he suggesting that people needed to transform their lives in operative ways that would lead them closer to God? In other words, was he challenging those in Hebrew society to have a change of heart? Possibly Jesus was saying that the kingdom of God was some future reality for which all of his followers need to prepare, a reality that society would one day see when he returned to reclaim the world. Could it be that Jesus actually founded the kingdom of God on earth, and was challenging those who heard him to do what they could in word and action to build the kingdom and make it more a positive reality for others? Certainly, Jesus's use of this term gives us more tools to better understand the Lord's question: "Who do you say that I am?"

Discussion Questions

1. Which aspect of Jesus's mission to the world do you find most attractive and why?
2. Do you believe Jesus's mission to the world was a success? What is necessary in our contemporary world for his message to find greater acceptance?
3. People often suggest that if Jesus walked into any of our churches today, he would not be recognized. How do you see the mission of Christ today? How is it manifested in today's world?
4. Which of Robert Stein's "schools" associated with the concept of the kingdom of God do you find most attractive and why?
5. Do you believe it is your responsibility to either bring about or make more present the kingdom of God on earth?

Chapter 9

INTERPRETING THE TEACHING OF JESUS

The basic question of this book, "Who do you say that I am?" can obviously be answered in many ways. The chapters in this monograph ask the reader to consider many different images and ideas. Speaking generally, the Lord has been seen as an object of faith or history. More specifically he can be described as a miracle worker, reverser of roles, or a God of compassion and mercy. Traditionally, one of the most profound images of Jesus is that he was a teacher. The central core of Christ's teaching is presented in Matthew 5—7, in the famous Sermon on the Mount, but Jesus's whole life, both actions and words, served to educate the people of his day, as they continue to do for contemporary twenty-first-century Christians. His miraculous cures, specific teachings to his apostles and other disciples, and even possibly most profoundly, the example he set, such as washing the feet of his disciples at the Last Supper (John 13:1–20), manifest the many ways that he was a teacher.

While Jesus clearly was a teacher in action and word, how one understands the ideas and precepts that he taught can certainly be understood in different ways. As we have seen, through an examination of his parables, the Gospels in general can be understood and have been interpreted in varied ways over time. Even today on any typical Sunday, preachers will present varied messages and understandings in their reading of the gospel message. Thus, it is important that we look at how the teachings of Jesus have been and can be interpreted by people of faith. If we are to answer the question Jesus put before Peter, we must have an understanding of Jesus's teaching and how it has applicability in today's world.

JESUS'S TEACHING ON THE FATHERHOOD OF GOD

It is clear that Jesus had a very close and intimate relationship with the Father. As stated previously, he referred to the Father as *Abba* (or "daddy"). This unique relationship is captured in a very powerful way in Matthew 11:25–27. The text reads,

> At that time Jesus said, "I thank you, Father, Lord of heaven and earth, because you have hidden these things from the wise and the intelligent and have revealed them to infants; yes, Father, for such was your gracious will. All things have been handed over to me by my Father; and no one knows the Son except the Father and no one knows the Father except the Son and anyone to whom the Son chooses to reveal him."

Jesus's use of the term *Abba* and his general linking of God with the person of "the Father," demonstrate a close and intimate relationship. Trust is complete between the Father and the Son, Jesus, in that the former hands all things over to the Son, with sufficient confidence that Jesus will do what is necessary in revealing God to others.

What does this intimate relationship between Jesus and the Father mean for his overall teaching and the quest of our overall investigation? Certainly, the close relationship between the Father and the Son speaks on a very human level, encouraging all followers of Jesus to have a similar relationship, both with the Father in heaven and in our various human relationships, whether that be with our parents and family or others we encounter along the road of life. Jesus is teaching his followers that God is not a stranger or one who is bent on revenge and punishment. Rather, the intimacy with which Jesus speaks about his Father tells us that we should have a similar intimacy. Jesus's relationship with God, his Father, sets, for most, an attractive view that we can trust God absolutely, for he will take care of us, and will provide for us as he did for his Son, Jesus. What God provides might not always be precisely what we want; challenges and various crosses will be part of our human journey. But if we believe that Jesus's teaching is true, we can also be confident that in the end we will find the glory that can only be attained in the presence of the Father.

JESUS'S ETHICAL TEACHING: HOW CAN IT BE UNDERSTOOD?

While it would be nice, simple, and certainly convenient to find a systematic approach to Jesus's teaching, the reality is that he, like St. Paul, never produced a "systematic theology" that provides his summary teaching on any particular subject. In fact, at times, it seems that Jesus's teachings are even contradictory. How can he say that he has come to fulfill the law, when on numerous occasions, he openly breaks the Mosaic Law on Sabbath observance and ritual purity? How can the "loving Jesus" who has such an intimate relationship with his Father say that he has come to bring division within a family, setting a father against his son and the mother against her daughter (Luke 12:52–53)? At times, what Jesus teaches, what he asks of his followers, is impossible to accomplish. How can Jesus expect us to follow his challenge, "If you wish to be perfect, go, sell your possessions, and give the money to the poor, and you will have treasure in heaven; then come, follow me" (Matt 19:21)?

Several other important questions arise with respect to the teachings of Jesus. For example, are Jesus's teachings meant to be universal, or are they limited to a certain group of people at a particular time? Does the timelessness of Scripture apply in all cases or are these teachings limited to a certain time period? Even more importantly, are the ethical teachings of Jesus understood as entrance requirements into the kingdom of God or are they rules for those who are already members of the kingdom? How have the ethical teachings of Jesus been understood in history and how are they understood today?

The biblical scholar Robert Stein, in *The Method and Message of Jesus' Teaching*, presents six different ways to interpret the teachings of Jesus in the Scriptures. His first perspective, what he calls the "Catholic Interpretation," suggests that the teachings of Jesus must be understood as a two-level ethic. He suggests that all followers of Christ must follow the basics of the faith, things like the Ten Commandments, the basic commandment to love, and the Golden Rule. The second, higher level, for those who desire to be "perfect," requires more. Basing his analysis on the early Christian tradition that those who willingly abandoned the world to more closely follow Christ, that is, priests and religious (therefore the name "Catholic Interpretation"), were choosing the higher or more "perfect" life, Stein suggests that Jesus's teachings that seem utopian and impossible are only intended for a select group. To surrender one's possessions, to deny family and marriage is not for everyone. This interpretation is popular with many, and not just Roman Catholics, because it says that salvation is open to all and it provides a clear goal that Christians should seek to attain. However, Stein proffers the opinion that this is not what Jesus taught.

Beyond the "Catholic Interpretation," Stein offers other perspectives. A second understanding, referred to as the "Utopian Interpretation," argues for a more literal adherence to Jesus's teachings. Stein suggests that this interpretation is certainly correct inasmuch as Jesus's teachings and commands were not addressed to a spiritual elite, but to all people. Some Christian groups, historically referred to in the post-Reformation era as radical reformers, such as Quakers, Mennonites, and the Amish, have adopted this view as the basic pattern for discipleship. Stein believes that Jesus was not suggesting the kingdom of God was a new community or radical departure from life, and, therefore, there is no need to remove oneself from the collective common Christian community.

A third perspective, the "Lutheran Interpretation," rejects the Catholic two-tiered understanding by suggesting that the Sermon on the Mount (Matt 5—7) is applicable to all. However, in opposition to the "Utopian Interpretation," this perspective suggests that the ethical demands of Jesus are unattainable. Thus, because humanity is not able to fulfill Jesus's commands, modern disciples of the Lord are challenged to live lives of faith in Christ, who alone can fulfill his own teaching. This interpretation reveals the brokenness and sinfulness of humanity, and thus the need for Christians to throw themselves on the mercy of God.

Stein's last three perspectives of Jesus's ethical teaching begin with the "Liberal Interpretation." This understanding sees Jesus's moral imperative to be concerned more with who people are rather than what they do. In other words, Jesus was more concerned with the eradication of what was in the human heart and its destructive power, than describing a specific form of ethical conduct one should manifest. We recall the words of Jesus: "Do you not see that whatever goes into a person from outside cannot defile....It is what comes out of a person that defiles" (Mark 7:18, 20). This interpretation views Jesus's commands as figurative, not literal.

A fifth perspective, the "Interim Ethic Interpretation," is closely associated with Albert Schweitzer (whom we recall from our study of the Historical Jesus), who believed Jesus's teaching to be eschatological, that is, oriented toward the end times, the second coming of Jesus. Under this interpretation the Sermon on the Mount was preached by Jesus to provide an interim ethic before the approaching *parousia*, or second coming. However, because Christ's return has not come quickly, this interpretation is impractical and should be rejected.

Stein's final understanding, the "Existential Interpretation," suggests that Jesus's teaching was not a system of rules for conduct, but rather an existential call for decision. Under this perspective, Jesus never intended his teaching to be an ethical system (*Method and Message,* 90–99).

INTERPRETING JESUS'S TEACHING ON RELATIONSHIPS

It is clear in the Bible that many of Jesus's ethical teachings presume a new relationship between the individual and God. It is clearly evident, for example, that the cost to be a disciple of Christ will indeed be high. Luke presents a good example:

> As they were going along the road, someone said to him, "I will follow you wherever you go." And Jesus said to him, "Foxes have holes, and birds of the air have nests; but the Son of Man has nowhere to lay his

> head.'" To another he said, "Follow me." But he said, "Lord, first let me go and bury my father." But Jesus said to him, "Let the dead bury their own dead; but as for you, go and proclaim the kingdom of God." Another said, "I will follow you, Lord; but let me first say farewell to those at my home." Jesus said to him, "No one who puts a hand to the plow and looks back is fit for the kingdom of God." (Luke 9:57–62)

Clearly, not only does Jesus mandate complete dedication to himself and his mission, but even, it seems, requires one to separate from one's family and friends. But what exactly is Jesus saying? Is not the Lord challenging his followers to place their priority with him, rather than the world, even one's family?

Jesus also emphasizes the need for *metanoia*, a change of heart. We recall the Lord's famous conversation with Nicodemus, a Pharisee and leader of the Jews, who came to Jesus at night. While Jesus's words to Nicodemus were confusing to the latter, the message to us must be clear: "Very truly, I tell you, no one can enter the kingdom of God without being born of water and Spirit. What is born of the flesh is flesh, and what is born of the Spirit is spirit. Do not be astonished that I said to you, 'You must be born from above'" (John 3:5–7). We see this as well in Jesus's encounter with Zacchaeus (Luke 19:1–10), which shows how Christ reached out to individuals, asking for the transformation of their heart.

Closely related to this new attitude of the transformation of one's heart is Jesus's command to love. Only when we love our neighbor can we truly love God. The believer is asked to love all, and not in limited ways. Speaking of the basic commandments, we read in Mark,

> Jesus answered, "The first is, 'Hear, O Israel: the Lord our God, the Lord is one; you shall love the Lord your

> God with all your heart, and with all your soul, and with all your mind, and with all your strength.' The second is this, 'You shall love your neighbor as yourself.' There is no other commandment greater than these." (Mark 12:29–31)

Jesus is equally clear in John's Gospel:

> I give you a new commandment, that you love one another. Just as I have loved you, you also should love one another. By this everyone will know that you are my disciples, if you have love for one another. (John 13:34–35)

Jesus's words are universal and noncompromising. Love, therefore, becomes a basic foundation block and tenet for interpretation of not only his teaching, but his mission in the world.

One might ask, considering Jesus's insistence on the demands of discipleship and the need to love, should we see this and all of his teaching as seeking reward or merit? Initially one might answer yes, saying, "We adhere to the teachings of Jesus today to find the reward of heaven tomorrow," but from a review of Scripture, it is not so obvious. For example, in the Sermon on the Mount Jesus says,

> So whenever you give alms, do not sound a trumpet before you, as the hypocrites do in the synagogues and in the streets, so that they may be praised by others. Truly I tell you, they have received their reward. But when you give alms, do not let your left hand know what your right hand is doing, so that your alms may be done in secret; and your Father who sees in secret will reward you. (Matt 6:2–4)

In a similar way, Luke reports Jesus saying,

> He said also to the one who had invited him, "When you give a luncheon or dinner, do not invite your friends or your brothers or your relatives or rich neighbors, in case they may invite you in return, and you be repaid. But when you give a banquet, invite the poor, the crippled, the lame, and the blind. And you will be blessed, because they cannot repay you, for you will be repaid at the resurrection of the righteous." (Luke 14:12–14)

While these passages are very clear, the answer to the question becomes cloudier when we read in Luke, "So you also, when you have done all that you were ordered to do, say, 'We are worthless slaves; we have done only what we ought to have done!'" (Luke 17:10). These confusing, seemingly contradictory statements by Jesus prompt us to ask in general why we choose to follow the Lord and why we might perform a specific act—to be rewarded or simply because it is the right thing to do? What is our motivation in following the teaching of Jesus and what does this say about how we answer the Lord's question, Who do you say that I am?

THE UNIQUENESS OF JESUS'S TEACHING

Jesus's teaching was powerful, wide-ranging, and certainly challenging, but how was it unique? First, and probably most profoundly, Jesus used the vehicle of parables as his principal method of teaching. Parables allowed him to present a wide range of moral imperatives in a way that was attractive to listeners. Jesus presented a story that was understandable, to which people could relate; and he did so in a way that was somewhat hidden. As he said when questioned about his use of parables, "To you has been given the secret of the kingdom of God, but for those outside, everything comes in parables; in order that 'they may indeed look, but not perceive, and may indeed listen, but not understand; so that they may not turn again and be forgiven'" (Mark 4:11–12).

Next, Jesus was a master at synthesizing his ideas. As a great teacher, Jesus understood that concepts need to be presented in a way that are not only succinct, but also understandable to those listening to the message. Jesus did not present long and complicated ideas, but rather spoke more directly and simply. Jesus's teaching was unique in that he cut away some of the Jewish traditions that had overgrown and thereby occluded the Word of God. Stripping away that which had complicated the issue addressed allowed people to better understand his message. Certainly, Jesus's message was much more positive. He did not dwell on the negative, but rather transformed negative situations and actions into teachable moments for those who followed him.

Besides the uniqueness of Jesus's teaching and its method, the content was in many ways equally revolutionary. Jesus placed more emphasis on the spirit of the law than its letter, emphasizing the need for one to be transformed internally so as to understand fully his message. Certainly, Jesus had a revolutionary attitude toward outcasts. For him the last would be first and the first would be last, masters should be servants, and those who had been totally rejected by society—lepers, Samaritans, women, and foreigners—were shown to be exemplars and more acceptable to God than those whom society considered to be the most important.

Lastly, but equally important, Jesus taught by his perfect example. When he washed the feet of his disciples (John 13:1–20), his strident words against the hypocrisy of the Pharisees and scribes, and certainly his voluntary action to undergo his passion and death without complaint, dramatically demonstrate the efficacy and power of his ability to teach by example.

JESUS'S SELF UNDERSTANDING

Our investigation of how to interpret Jesus's teaching cannot conclude without a serious review of what Jesus taught about himself. To begin, one might ask, what did Jesus's actions say about him? First, Christ seemed to claim special authority. Mark 11:27–33 reads,

> Again they came to Jerusalem. As he was walking in the temple, the chief priests, the scribes, and the elders came to him and said, "By what authority are you doing these things? Who gave you this authority to do them?" Jesus said to them, "I will ask you one question; answer me, and I will tell you by what authority I do these things. Did the baptism of John come from heaven, or was it of human origin? Answer me." They argued with one another, "If we say, 'From heaven,' he will say, 'Why then did you not believe him?' But shall we say, 'Of human origin'?"—they were afraid of the crowd, for all regarded John as truly a prophet. So they answered Jesus, "We do not know." And Jesus said to them, "Neither will I tell you by what authority I am doing these things."

Jesus claimed authority over demons, such as those calling themselves "Legion" (Mark 5:1–20); he claimed authority to perform miracles. Jesus also claimed divine prerogative, not only by performing many supernatural miracles—curing people of illness, raising the dead, and even controlling the weather—but also the power to forgive sins. Mark writes, "When Jesus saw their faith, he said to the paralytic, 'Son, your sins are forgiven.' Now some of the scribes were sitting there, questioning in their hearts, 'Why does this fellow speak in this way? It is blasphemy! Who can forgive sins but God alone?'" (Mark 2:5–7).

Jesus also claimed authority over the Sabbath. Luke relates the following story:

> Now he was teaching in one of the synagogues on the sabbath. And just then there appeared a woman with a spirit that had crippled her for eighteen years. She was bent over and was quite unable to stand up straight. When Jesus saw her, he called her over and said, "Woman, you are set free from your ailment." When he laid his hands on her, immediately she stood up straight and began praising God. But the leader of the synagogue, indignant because Jesus had cured on the sabbath, kept saying to the crowd, "There are six days on which work ought to be done; come on those days and be cured, and not on the sabbath day." But the Lord answered him and said, "You hypocrites! Does not each of you on the sabbath untie his ox or his donkey from the manger, and lead it away to give it water? And ought not this woman, a daughter of Abraham whom Satan bound for eighteen long years, be set free from this bondage on the sabbath day?" (Luke 13:10–16)

Lastly, Jesus claimed the freedom to intensify, reverse, or even annul the law. For example, speaking of the sin of adultery, Jesus said that if one looks lustfully at another, one is also guilty (Matt 5:28). He seemed to reverse the law when he said, "The sabbath was made for humankind, and not humankind for the sabbath; so the Son of Man is lord even of the sabbath" (Mark 2:27–28). He certainly muted the law and its efficacy by suggesting that compassion, as exhibited in the action of the Good Samaritan, was more important than maintenance of the law, as seen in the inaction of the priest and the Levite (Luke 10:25–37).

Jesus's self-understanding through his proclamations of authority are seen in other areas as well. He claimed a totalitarian view of obedience and response to him. Speaking both to his disciples and a collected crowd, Jesus said,

> If any want to become my followers, let them deny themselves and take up their cross and follow me. For those who want to save their life will lose it, and those who lose their life for my sake, and for the sake of the gospel, will save it. For what will it profit them to gain the whole world and forfeit their life? Indeed, what can they give in return for their life? Those who are ashamed of me and of my words in this adulterous and sinful generation, of them the Son of Man will also be ashamed when he comes in the glory of his Father with the holy angels. (Mark 8:34–38)

Jesus also claimed that the fate of humanity revolved around him. He stated, "Do not think that I have come to abolish the law or the prophets; I have come not to abolish but to fulfill" (Matt 5:17). Again he said, "Come to me, all you that are weary and are carrying heavy burdens, and I will give you rest. Take my yoke upon you, and learn from me; for I am gentle and humble in heart, and you will find rest for your souls. For my yoke is easy, and my burden is light" (Matt 11:28–30). Going further, Jesus proclaimed, "Those who are well have no need of a physician, but those who are sick; I have come to call not the righteous but sinners" (Mark 2:17). Lastly, he claimed superiority over the "Saints" of the Old Testament. When challenged by the Pharisees that he and his disciples had violated the law, Jesus replied, "I tell you, something greater than the temple is here" (Matt 12:6).

Our review of Jesus's self-understanding can conclude by describing the many titles that he claimed. In Matthew 16:16, Peter answers Jesus's question—the question of this book, "Who do you say that I am?"—by revealing that Jesus is the Messiah. Later, when Jesus stands before the high priest and the Jewish religious hierarchy, he accepts the title "Messiah," claiming "I am" (Mark 14:62). While not unique to the New Testament, Jesus's claim to be the Son of God was qualitatively more important in degree and in kind than references in the Hebrew Bible (Old Testament) that equate "Son of God" to angels and Israel. Besides Messiah and Son of God, Jesus's favorite self-title was "Son of Man," which is found sixty-nine times in the Synoptics and thirteen times in John. The frequency of this title and that Jesus uses it to describe himself testify to its importance. The title has three different understandings in the New Testament. First, Son of Man references Jesus's earthly ministry as seen in Mark: "'But so that you may know that the Son of Man has authority on earth to forgive sins'—he said to the paralytic—'I say to you, stand up, take your mat and go to your home'" (Mark 2:10–11). Next, the title refers to the future suffering, death, and resurrection of Jesus. Later on, Mark writes, "Then he began to teach them that the Son of Man must undergo great suffering, and be rejected by the elders, the chief priests, and the scribes, and be killed, and after three days rise again" (Mark 8:31).

Lastly, Jesus's favorite personal title refers to his glorious return: "When they persecute you in one town, flee to the next; for truly I tell you, you will not have gone through all the towns of Israel before the Son of Man comes" (Matt 10:23).

CONCLUSION

Our investigation of Jesus's classic question to Peter, "Who do you say that I am?" can, as we have suggested in an earlier chapter, be answered in part by suggesting that he was a great teacher. To say this, however, is insufficient unless we understand and can in some way interpret what Jesus taught. The Lord certainly had a personal relationship with God that gave him a great platform from which to teach, but there must be much more to our interpretation. Scholars have interpreted Jesus's ethical teaching in varied ways, from a literalist perspective to one that has no application to contemporary life, and several intermediate gradations between these polar opposites. The Bible clearly shows that Jesus's teaching was in many ways unique. His use of parables with their polyvalent meaning was central to his method. In his message he concluded that followers must pay a high price and seek a transformation of heart to be true disciples. Jesus's revolutionary attitude toward outcasts and his exemplary way of life were other unique aspects of his pedagogical style. In his role as teacher, Jesus claimed special authority, including divine prerogative, giving him the freedom to alter the Mosaic Law, a central tenet of Jewish society. Lastly, in order to properly interpret the teaching of Jesus, we must understand the various titles—Messiah, Son of God, and Son of Man—that the Lord used for himself. Having a better grasp on the interpretation of Jesus's teaching has, hopefully, aided our overall quest. We must next investigate the role of Jesus as a moral decision maker, for indeed many would suggest this was the primary legacy he left for all of his followers.

Discussion Questions

1. Why do you think Jesus was so attractive to many as a teacher?
2. How do you understand Jesus's challenge to personal transformation? What might this entail for you?

3. Since many of Jesus's teachings seem to contradict the prevailing wisdom of his day, why do you think people who heard him considered his ideas to be authoritative?
4. Which of Jesus's teachings methods is most attractive to you? Why?
5. What can you learn about yourself and your Christian vocation from the teachings of Jesus?

Chapter 10

JESUS, THE MORAL DECISION MAKER

As we learned in the previous chapter, and as many might expect, the teaching of Jesus can be understood and interpreted in various ways. The timelessness of the parables as his principal method of teaching, combined with his (at times) indirect words, often present a conundrum to readers of the Gospels, both scholars and ordinary faith-filled Christians. One thing is certain, however. Many of Jesus's teachings, in whatever form they took, can be classified under the general category of morals. From the dawn of human civilization, moral decision-making has been endemic to society. We make various kinds of moral decisions, some rather simple and others much more profound, almost on a daily basis. A tendency can easily arise to equate moral decisions with sexuality, but this is only one subset of a much broader and more involved genre of decisions. When decisions are made that benefit one group or individual to the detriment of the common good, a moral injustice arises. When individuals alone or in groups, including companies, make decisions to skirt the rules in order to become more profitable, again a moral injustice has been perpetrated. In the most contemporary of scenarios, when issues such as refugee and immigration policies, racial profiling, or the basic human rights established in the Declaration of Independence and the Constitution arise, the question of moral decision-making comes front and center.

As we continue our study of how to answer Jesus's classic question, "Who do you say that I am?" we must ask what relevance Jesus's life and mission as a moral decision maker has on our response. Does Jesus set moral imperatives that must never be crossed, or does he provide standards that Christians must strive to attain? What can Jesus's teaching about the moral life add to the answers we seek to formulate about him? Since Jesus's moral exhortations and teachings were so central to his ministry, it is appropriate and necessary to take an in-depth look at Jesus as a moral decision maker.

THE MORAL LEGACY OF JESUS

While the Gospels are filled with examples of Jesus's various moral teachings, what is the relationship between what Jesus taught and what religious belief professes? Are Jesus's instructions in the moral life the same as what Christianity teaches, or are there differences? More importantly, how great is the contrast between the exhortations of Jesus (assuming these to be the same as Christian belief) and the morality of those who profess to be Christians and thus consider his teachings to be of the utmost importance? Certainly, all people, including all Christians, are sinners, and therefore do not fully measure up to the Christian ideal, but what is the power of the moral legacy of Jesus?

The above questions reignite an earlier debate in this book on the authority of the teachings of Jesus. In a previous chapter, we explored the idea of whether the general teachings of Jesus are an expectation for his followers, or an ideal to which Christians should aspire, with the knowledge that they will never achieve such a lofty, almost utopian, goal. If one sees the teachings of Jesus, including his moral missives, as norms for the Christian faithful, then one must conclude that the moral teaching of Jesus does not have a great legacy. On the other hand, if one views the teaching of Jesus as a utopian goal, then the fact that Christians seek to follow any and all of his teachings, including his moral message, suggests that Jesus's moral legacy is strong.

It seems, then, that the moral legacy of Jesus is mostly dependent on one's interpretation of his teaching. This interpretation is largely formed through published literature in the field, but most especially from personal experience. As the expression goes, "experience is the greatest teacher." Indeed, what we know about the moral life of Jesus is found in Scripture. How that has been interpreted by scholarly literature must be lived out, on a day-to-day basis, by the average Christian. It is through experience that we learn lifelong lessons, teachings that when compared with the specifics of Jesus's teaching provide us with an interpretation and allow us to apply the Lord's message in our daily lives. Surely, the application of Jesus's teaching in all things, but possibly most especially in the moral life, should be the goal that all Christians strive to attain. Clearly, Scripture does not provide a specific teaching of the Lord on every moral question, but the basic principles are present, and through their application to real life, can be useful in the challenges of morality and faith that come our way on almost a daily basis.

Jesus's teaching in all areas serves as an example of what we should do. Essentially, we are to seek to conform ourselves to Christ. But what precisely does this mean? To conform one's self to Christ means that we should follow his action in our lives. In other words, Jesus becomes a pattern of life for those who seek to follow him. Certainly, Jesus is the perfect example, the one who should always be imitated. Jesus was the one who gave the best example of obedience. Immediately after the Last Supper, before his arrest by the Roman cohort, Jesus went to the

Garden of Gethsemane, praying, "My Father, if it is possible, let this cup pass from me; yet not what I want but what you want" (Matt 26:39). Jesus knew his fate, probably to minute detail, but he obediently went forward to complete the Father's will. He gave the perfect example of suffering, carrying out the prophecy of the "Servant" described by Isaiah, one who would allow others to beat him and pluck his beard, one who would not revolt against buffets and spitting, but rather would persevere through all such humiliation and willingly suffer for others. Jesus was the perfect example of humility. When he, the Master, washed the feet of his disciples (John 13:1–20), he provided the best example of humbly reaching out in the service of others. In short, Jesus is the physical revelation of the action of the unseen God. When one sees the example of Jesus, one understands the desire of God.

Christians, those who seek to follow the moral teaching of Jesus, are exhorted to imitate his passion and mortification. The morally serious Christian possesses the perfect example of the ideal life when he observes the life, mission, and message of Jesus. Jesus becomes a pattern for self-denial and self-sacrifice. He shows those who wish to follow him what is truly necessary to be a disciple. Through his example, the Lord shows us a life lived in love and service to others. While some see Jesus as the perfect example, others may see him as a moral ideal. Either way, however, it cannot be denied that Jesus is the perfect example and pattern for life.

What precisely was Jesus's pattern or blueprint for life? The answer must begin with the reality that the Christian life is one of discipleship, which if lived well, comes at a high price. Indeed, the well-known Lutheran pastor and theologian Dietrich Bonhoeffer, in his famous book *The Cost of Discipleship*, expresses the reality that when Christ calls one, he calls that individual to die. It may not be a physical death of martyrdom, as Bonhoeffer himself experienced, but it must be a life of great sacrifice, giving of oneself for the betterment of others, especially for the common good. Discipleship leads to actions and attitudes that are distinctly ethical and moral. It also leads to a pattern of self-denial, the goal of which is the utopian ideal of perfection.

JESUS THE MORAL TEACHER

What precisely is the authority of Jesus on moral questions? While (as stated above) some might see Jesus's teachings as absolutes, recent biblical scholarship has raised some questions about the timelessness of applying his teachings to contemporary life. One of the main difficulties associated with the Bible in general, and, therefore, his moral teaching, is how much we can precisely know about the words and actions of Jesus. Biblical criticism and exegesis can only go so far. Associated more with the Jesus of history, as we recall Marcus Borg's "emerging paradigm" theology, biblical scholars for the last fifty to sixty years have sought to see Jesus as one who made God known, not as one who brought an ideal pattern of life or a moral code.

If Jesus truly is the ideal pattern and moral code for life, then what ought we, his followers, do, and what does this mean about the basic question this book hopes to answer, "Who do you say that I am?" Some would suggest that we should follow Jesus's teaching, for it is in accord with God's purpose and intention in our life. God has loved us into existence and wants us to return home. Thus, we have been given, in the life and message of Jesus, the perfect pattern, the ideal example to follow. Others, however, would suggest using Jesus as an ideal, that God trusts us as adults and thus we must use our own free will to generate a personal moral code. Through this understanding, we seek to follow Christ as we would best understand him. Still others would suggest that a personal moral code is too amorphous and can lead, as they say, down the "slippery slope," especially with respect to moral decision-making. Some suggest that Jesus's moral teachings are norms, are authoritative, and determine our choices. In this case we have no options. In this view, we follow Jesus closely today to find eternal life tomorrow. Lastly, there are still a few others for whom Jesus's teaching provides a basic direction for the moral life.

Jesus's role as a moral teacher calls all who seek to follow him to a radical obedience of self-sacrifice and love. Pragmatically speaking this means that all Christians must have a willingness to be obedient to God's will. We are, again as Bonhoeffer suggests, not to count the cost but rather to obediently go forward and with persistent energy walk the road of discipleship. This path requires a willingness to be obedient; for many Christians Jesus not only commands, but equally if not more importantly, points us in the proper direction.

Again, as we described when discussing Jesus as the "reverser of roles," we recall that Christ brought a new law. In fulfilling the law, Jesus brought its spirit, its rationale. He taught a paradigm of compassion rather than strict adherence to the Mosaic Law. Still, many contemporary moral theologians are reluctant to say that Jesus's teaching provides a new moral norm. Yet at the same time they cannot deny the authority of his teaching. Some Protestant theologians may have some difficulty with Jesus's new law, since Luther found the law to be an obstacle to his battle cry, "*sola fide*," justification by faith alone. But Catholic moral theologians, following the example of St. Thomas Aquinas, see Jesus's new law encapsulated in his "Sermon on the Mount." Specifically, this means adherence to the Golden Rule, and living a life of *agape*, that is, of service to our brothers and sisters.

CHRIST AND THE MORAL LIFE

Is there a systematic way to address the question of the influence that Jesus Christ has on the Christian moral life? A famous story about the Indian freedom fighter Mahatma Gandhi addresses this question in a powerful way. Gandhi was a Hindu, but he was very familiar with the Bible and often read it. One day, the story goes, he was on a train and someone asked him, "Mr. Gandhi, I wonder with your knowledge of the Bible and its message if you would ever be inclined to convert to Christianity and follow the way of Jesus." Gandhi answered, "The message of the Bible is powerful, and Jesus's example is indeed one to follow, and I would seriously consider doing so. The only problem is I have never actually met someone who truly is a Christian." Gandhi's challenging words should prompt us to ask what the actual influence of Christ has been on those who claim to be his followers.

Biblical scholars and moral theologians have addressed this issue. The famous twentieth-century Swiss Protestant theologian Karl Barth (1886–1968) suggests that many Christians are put to shame by others whose moral lives are more Christian than those who profess to be Jesus's contemporary disciples. If those claiming the name "Christian" live lives inconsistent with Jesus's mission and message, then Barth suggests Christians are in no position to claim any moral authority or superiority. They can only really claim certain attitudes and intentions that are moral and demonstrate character. Moral theologian James Gustafson suggests that Jesus Christ often can make, ought to make, and many times does make a difference in the moral lives of those in the Christian community. For him, Christians have a common object of loyalty, namely Jesus, the one who reveals God (the Father) in bodily form. It is Christ who gives Christians a certain posture and perspective toward life. For example, because of Jesus's triumph over evil, one can have a fundamental confidence in the world. It is Jesus who makes possible the confidence that one has in the power and presence of God. The Bible testifies to how God can be trusted even when people have failed him. Thus, for Gustafson, Jesus manifests the moral pattern all should follow if they seek to truly be his disciples. Gustafson's ideas suggest that Jesus gives to all his followers a certain disposition on life, an attitude toward the world. Like all peoples, Christians tend to be creatures of habit, and therefore have a persistent tendency to act in a certain way. He also argues that people, through their actions, can have a lasting disposition that manifests loyalty to Christ.

The work of the above-mentioned scholars must be understood in the light of the hope that only Christ can bring. During his public ministry Jesus constantly brought hope and light to those in despair and darkness. Christians need to be predisposed to this same hope. Hope relates to the goodness of God; it is grounded in one's trust in the Lord. The expression of old is true, "Hope springs eternal." In the biblical sense, the author of the Book of Proverbs (3:5) succinctly and powerfully describes where our trust and hope must be:

> "Trust in the LORD with all your heart,
> and do not rely on your own insight."

The hope that Christ brings through our trust in him must be a shining light that guides the moral compass of our lives.

The Christian moral life, as Christ proclaimed and lived it, must be a centerpiece of our life of discipleship. The Christian perspective on life, governed by loyalty to Christ, must form in all contemporary disciples certain intentions. It must manifest certain governing purposes in life. In other words, the Christian moral perspective must provide a certain direction, one that leads home to God and life eternal. Jesus provides this normative Christian theological interpretation of God's place in one's life. Hence he is the perfect paradigm for what people should do in any particular situation. Disciples of Jesus are obliged to consider Christ as the most important norm among others in all judgments and actions. Indeed, Jesus is the norm that illuminates options and deeply conditions any and all choices. While Jesus does not confine us, prescribing certain options and eliminating other choices, he must be the norm for the Christian in leading the moral life.

CONCLUSION

Our quest to answer Jesus's classic question, "Who do you say that I am?" has prompted us to look to the Lord as a great teacher of the moral life. Christians must rightly ask what the legacy of Jesus is, especially when we consider the too often inconsistent behavior found between what Jesus and his followers claim, and what the manifest behavior of ordinary Christians actually is. The challenge for the Christian is to be conformed to Christ, to see him as a pattern of life that should be imitated in any and all ways. We have learned that Jesus insisted his followers live a life of discipleship, a pattern of life presenting distinctly ethical attitudes and actions consistent with those the Lord demonstrated during his public ministry. Jesus truly is the moral teacher par excellence. While some would suggest that Christians should follow Jesus's teaching as a response to the God who first loved us, others might proclaim that Christ's public ministry manifests norms and is authoritative in the determination of choices. For others, Jesus's moral teachings and exhortations provide a basic direction for life. Clearly, Jesus brought a new law whose spirit was encapsulated in the Golden Rule of the New Testament and *agape*, a Greek word that refers to a life of service. In the end, Jesus gives a certain disposition on life and attitude toward the world, one that brings hope if only we will trust God sufficiently.

Investigating the idea of Jesus as a moral teacher adds many tools to our overall bag of instruments as we attempt to answer the Lord's question to Peter. For some, the basic answer may be that Jesus is indeed the moral standard by which we can evaluate our own life. For others, the role of Jesus as moral teacher may simply serve as one factor to a more complicated response. In formulating our answer, we must next ask, what is the association of Jesus and his teaching to contemporary culture? Therefore let us turn to an analysis of this question, asking how this relationship can help us answer the question, "Who do you say that I am?"

Discussion Questions

1. Do you see Jesus's moral teachings as imperative for life, or simply lofty utopian goals that we should seek, but believe they never can be fully implemented?
2. What does the virtue of hope mean to you? How has it been significant in your life?
3. For you, what is the greatest moral legacy of Jesus?
4. What does Gandhi's challenge to properly live the Christian life say to you?
5. What does Jesus's pattern of life say about the way you live your life?

Chapter 11

JESUS AND CONTEMPORARY CULTURE

While our investigation of Jesus's classic question to Peter, "Who do you say that I am?" has taken us along various paths and helped us to understand the multiple dimensions of Christ, one thing is certainly clear. Jesus was an individual who clashed, sometimes even violently, with the culture of his day. If we see Jesus as a "reverser of roles," who said and did things directly opposed to what was normative in his day, the clash with his then-contemporary culture is obvious. His insistence that compassion was more important than the Mosaic Law; his outreach to those who stood on society's margins; his insistence that if you want to be acceptable to God, you need to humble yourself and sit at the lower end of the table; as well as his challenge to the authority of the religious elite were all actions or attitudes that placed him at odds with the cultural norms of his day. Jesus wasn't concerned with what people thought about his words and actions; rather, he valiantly and stridently did what he needed to do and said what was necessary in any and all situations.

Jesus's lack of concern for the prevailing wisdom of his day has been, and continues to be, a source of challenge and inspiration for those who bear the name "Christian." In the dark days of the Roman Empire until the conversion of Constantine, Christians, despite the fact that their discovery might lead to death, bucked against the Roman law to worship and to abide as much as possible in the teachings of Jesus, including the famous Golden Rule—loving God and loving our neighbor as ourselves. Constantine's conversion brought Christianity out of the shadows and greater acceptance within society, but conflict with culture never completely abated. The post–French Revolution era of history has once again, unfortunately, forced Christianity into the shadows. To be a true Christian today necessitates one to live counterculturally. With Christianity and culture so often in conflict, followers of Jesus must summon the strength, courage, and support they need to stand against the tide of secularism, living in a manner that might not be in the mainstream, but is the only life pattern that brings one home to God. Thus, a more in-depth exploration of the relationship of Jesus to culture will certainly benefit us in seeking the answer to our question.

THE ENDURING PROBLEM

What is the relationship between Christianity (and thus Jesus Christ) and culture? This fundamental question, which has endured throughout Christian history, has its roots in the life of Jesus himself. Even a brief overview of the Gospels, as described in an earlier chapter, shows how Jesus continually challenged the culture of his day. As a reverser of roles, turning things on their heads, Jesus seemed to ignore everything associated with the prevailing norms of his civilization and culture. He continually challenged authority, especially the religious elite of his day. Rather than simply falling in line and doing what everyone else did, Jesus "pushed the envelope," accusing the scribes and Pharisees of being hypocrites, especially regarding the inconsistency between their words and actions. He challenged the prevailing norms by saying that the last will be first and the first will be last; that if one wishes to be important, one must be the servant of all; and those that exalt themselves will be humbled, while those humbling themselves will be exalted. In place of the day's norms, Jesus preached an alternative wisdom where the traditional understanding of the centrality of the Mosaic Law became secondary to the practice of compassion, a wisdom that recognized the "little guy" in society to be as integral to the overall whole as the rich and the famous.

The sensation that Jesus caused in his lifetime by challenging his contemporary culture is still found today. It is increasingly the case today that many view Christianity as a hurdle, an obstacle, or even a hindrance to contemporary society's progress. The reason for this opinion is that orthodox Christian thought attacks many of the "sacred cows" of contemporary society. The perceived disconnect between Christianity and modern culture has only grown greater in the last twenty years. Issues that, in the past, were not found on the "radar screens" of the average person have today become frontline concerns, and even in some cases, the law of the land. Christianity is seen by some as depriving social institutions of elements that define their character. For some, Christianity challenges social unity and is therefore a hindrance to the advance of our society. The moral compass of Christianity is today generally viewed to be "problematic." Many even find Christ's radical forgiveness, going so far as to forgive those responsible for his Crucifixion, irreconcilable with the demands of contemporary justice. In short, Christianity is countercultural, a reality that seems to place Jesus at odds with our contemporary world.

Believers themselves may also have difficulties with the clash between Jesus and culture. Many modern Christians find it difficult to juxtapose Jesus's claims and his teaching with the demands society places on us, regardless of our faith practice. Thus, Christians find themselves trying to walk the narrow path between what appears to be the oppositional poles of Christ and culture. Pushed by both, the contemporary Christian experiences the daily challenge to successfully live in a society moving increasingly further from the Christian norm, while also seeking to hold close to the dictates and teachings of Christ, seeing them as the one and only path to life. The words of Jesus ring in our ears, "I am the way, and the truth, and the life. No one comes to the Father except through me" (John 14:6).

THE "PROBLEM" OF CHRIST AND CULTURE

The "problem" of placing Christ in our contemporary culture is an important issue for our overall quest in this book. In order to answer Jesus's question to Peter, we must have a firm grasp on how to view the mission of Jesus in our contemporary world. Is the message of Jesus a roadblock to the progress of contemporary society? Or, instead, is his mission an antidote to the "slippery slope" mentality of increasing relativism and situational ethics with respect to almost all issues? Understanding the various ways that Christ can be viewed in relationship to contemporary society is, therefore, an important element of our investigation.

Fortunately, this question has been analyzed through the seminal work of the famous Protestant theologian H. Richard Niebuhr (1894–1962) in his 1951 monograph, *Christ and Culture*. Niebuhr postulates three basic ideas. First, he speaks of Christ *against* culture. In this view, Jesus appears to be in opposition to the customs, culture, and society that contemporary

Christians experience. Next, he speaks of Christ *of* culture. Here he recognizes that there is a fundamental agreement between Christ and culture, that the apparent disconnect is a mirage, not a reality. Third, Niebuhr posits the idea of Christ *above* culture, the perspective that what Jesus says and does always trumps the dictates of contemporary society.

Beyond these three basic "solutions," Niebuhr suggests two other possibilities. The idea of Christ and culture in paradox suggests that both the authority of Jesus and culture are recognized, but the reality that they are in opposition is also accepted. In this case, Christians are subject to the tension accompanying two seemingly different authorities that don't agree, yet both must be obeyed simultaneously. In this view Christians are subjects of two worlds that are not discontinuous, but largely opposed. Lastly, Niebuhr suggests that Christ can be the *transformer* of culture. In this perspective, the fallen nature of humanity is acknowledged. Thus the power and presence of Jesus is actually necessary to transform society.

Niebuhr initiates his investigation by defining the two basic concepts in his examination, namely Jesus Christ and culture. As we have discovered in this volume, for many Jesus is seen as a teacher; many others see him as a lawgiver who promotes the spirit rather than the letter of the law. For others, Jesus is the revelation of God, the physical manifestation of God sent into the world. Others, still, see Jesus as the founder of the Church. For many the roles of Jesus are secondary to the virtues he manifested, with love being central and primary. Other virtues spring from this basic concept of love. He was a man of hope, one who was radically obedient to the point of death, and one of great humility. For those who emphasize virtue, it was Jesus's extreme faith that above all characterized his life. For Christ's followers, his example must be the basic pattern that they must follow in their lives. Niebuhr defines culture as the artificial secondary environment that humanity imposes on nature. This comprises language, habits, beliefs, customs, and values. Culture is a social heritage that society both receives and transmits to future generations. It is associated with both the temporal and material worlds, and it is pluralistic.

The first of Niebuhr's basic "solutions," *Christ against culture*, views Jesus as the sole authority over the Christian. This view rejects all claims of loyalty that culture would mandate, making Jesus the only one to whom the Christian would hold fidelity. This view is logical in many ways for it follows the basic Christian principle that Jesus is Lord of the universe and therefore the one in whom we place our trust, and to whom we profess our faithfulness. Additionally, this "solution" that Niebuhr offers has priority of precedence from a historical perspective. Early Christian writers spoke of, and average people lived their faith, as a way of life quite separate from culture. Jesus's radical approach to many of the standard cultural norms of his day set a pattern for those who would follow in his footsteps. Christians viewed themselves as a separate group from monotheistic Jews and polytheistic Gentiles. The understanding of God as one, but at the same time *triune*, set them apart from all others.

The Patristic era of Christian history provides additional historical evidence to the viability of this perspective. Christians were viewed as outcasts in Roman society due to several issues associated with their newfound faith. They were politically indifferent, seeing Rome's rule as some temporary reality on the road to the eternal kingship of Christ. The Christian view of chastity and marriage, as well as the refusal of Jesus's followers to enter military service, based on the belief that Jesus was a pacifist[1] were also problematic. Lastly, some Christians were seen as magicians or sorcerers leading the people to believe in the divinity of a crucified common criminal. This view of Christians led to numerous persecutions, both locally and empire-wide, on several occasions. The Emperors Nero (64–66), Domitian (95), Trajan (111), Marcus Aurelius (161–80), and Septimus Severus

(202–3) all waged local persecutions of Christians. The most infamous was Nero's accusation that Christians were responsible for Rome's burning. General persecutions throughout the empire were waged by the Emperors Decius (249–51), Valerian (258–60), and Diocletian (303–5).

After Constantine's "Edict of Tolerance" (311), which allowed all people to worship freely, Christianity continued to advocate a "Christ against culture" perspective with the dawn of monasticism. Starting with the anchorites, such as St. Anthony of the Desert (251–356), and the cenobites, such as St. Pachomius the Great (292–348), monasticism became formalized with the work and Rule of St. Benedict of Nursia (480–547) and his first community formed at Monte Cassino in the early sixth century. These men intentionally lived away from society and civilization in the belief that the true path to eternal life could be best found by absolute rejection of contemporary society. Later, during the Protestant Reformation, the Radical Reformers, also known pejoratively as the Anabaptists, continued to espouse this view. Today some of their religious ancestors can be seen in how the Amish, Mennonites, and Quakers, as three contemporary Christian groups, place Christ over culture.

In order to offer a balanced view, Niebuhr presents some theological problems associated with this perspective. First, he suggests that this "solution" denigrates reason and the work of the Enlightenment. Revelation is viewed as the only possible avenue of approach when judging the relationship between Christ and culture. Next, while nature, and therefore culture, is infested with sin, the Christian's role should be to pass from sin's darkness to salvation's light. Thus to avoid culture is inconsistent with the Christian call to transform the world. Today we might see this as the Christian's role to live in the world, but not of the world, viewing the world as a necessary reality, but not necessarily "buying in" to all its very popular and attractive trappings. Critics of this view also suggest that such a position neglects grace's significance, that the power of Christ can overcome any and all adversity. Lastly, this view contradicts the idea presented by St. John in his Gospel Prologue, that Jesus along with the Father is the Creator of nature. We read, "In the beginning was the Word, and the Word was with God, and the Word was God. He was in the beginning with God. All things came into being through him, and without him not one thing came into being" (John 1:1–3).

Niebuhr's second "solution" speaks of the "Christ of culture," that Jesus is the perfect fulfillment of culture's hopes and aspirations. In this viewpoint, no tension is perceived between Christ and the world; they harmonize together perfectly. Here Niebuhr is suggesting that there is no combative element between Christ and society, but rather that the two work together for the betterment and advancement of all. Historically, this perspective has been the model for some significant scholars. During the Medieval period, Peter Abelard (1079–1142) suggested that Christ was one who proclaimed his message and performed his works, both miracles and compassion, in the spirit that sought to find harmony with contemporary culture. During the Enlightenment this view was expressed by the famous English philosopher John Locke (1632–1704) in his 1695 treatise *The Reasonableness of Christianity*. Today, using this view, Christ is identified with what people conceived to be their finest ideals, most notable institutions, and best philosophies. In other words, Christ is imbued with all that is the best that society and culture can offer. Proponents of this view could appropriately be labeled "cultural Christians."

As with the first solution, critics of the "Christ of culture" concept are present. For some, those who hold this view tend to separate reason and revelation, with the former taking the high road and the latter taking the low or less significant road. Critics also claim that this view, which would see Jesus as the great teacher of rational truth and goodness, is a misinterpretation of his role in the world.

Niebuhr's third major "solution," that of "Christ above culture," is basically a synthesis argument confessing that Jesus is Lord of both the physical world and the spiritual, unseen, and intangible world. In this perspective, there can be reconciliation between the message of the gospel and the spirit of the contemporary world. Historically, the great champion of this view would be St. Thomas Aquinas (1225–74), who tried to combine Christian culture with the world by a form of Christianization of culture. St. Thomas's synthesis is attractive, for it seeks and discovers what is good in the nature of both humanity and the world. Additionally, seeking some synthesis, some sort of reconciliation between Christ and culture, is attractive to many.

Critics of this perspective perceive its compromise position as illusory and impractical. Rather than simply taking one side or the other, critics suggest that this middle position actually satisfies no one in its attempt to satisfy everyone. Critics suggest that this position simply seeks to prevent alienation of others, but in the process abandons the strengths of the two opposing views.

After explaining the three basic solutions to the question of Jesus's relationship to contemporary culture, Niebuhr closes his monograph with two other significant ideas that play into his overall analysis. First, he addresses the concept of Christ and culture in paradox. Using the basic definition that a paradox is a statement or a question that on first examination appears false but on closer scrutiny is found to be true, this perspective seeks to do justice by holding Christ and culture together while distinguishing between loyalty to Christ and responsibility for culture. In other words, Niebuhr suggests that while it appears that loyalty to Christ and responsibility for culture can never be simultaneously maintained, the reality is that they can both be held at the same time. He provides a couple of examples. First, he mentions the apparent opposition between law and grace. Why, he asks, cannot these two concepts work together as opposed to going in opposite directions? A second example is both the divine wrath and mercy of God. These two ideas are viewed by many to be at odds. Yet the Lord demonstrates both wrath, as with his condemnation of the scribes and Pharisees (Mark 7:1–16 being one example), and mercy, such as the compassion shown to the woman caught in the act of adultery (John 8:2–11).

This view was manifested in the work of St. Paul, who never attempted to remove himself or his followers from the cultural world in which he lived. Rather than living in an isolated community, Paul went out to the Gentiles, supporting them in every conceivable way, including winning a major victory at the Council of Jerusalem.[2] In his letters Paul speaks of a new life in Christ that he enjoyed and that others can equally experience. Immersed in the culture of his time, Paul saw no conflict between the teachings of Jesus and the Gentile world that could not be bridged. This perspective and ethic were lived in the midst of a society very often shrouded in darkness.

Niebuhr closes his analysis by looking at Christ as the *transformer* of culture. Proponents of this perspective hold fast to the radical distinction between God's work in Christ and man's work in culture. Rather than taking the more exclusive path of isolating Christianity from civilization, however, they view Jesus and his mission as the antidote. When engaging culture, Jesus's message and ethic, expressed in words and actions, can still transform culture. Proponents do not seek to modify Jesus's sharp critique of the world and its ways, but rather hold the view that for God all things are possible. Only Jesus can transform society in ways that will bring out culture's best aspects, and only he can utilize them effectively to build up the kingdom of God in our world.

CONCLUSION

Answering the question of our investigation, "Who do you say that I am?" requires one to ponder the relationship of Jesus to contemporary culture. This is an enduring problem present from the dawn of Christianity. Jesus's countercultural attitude and actions, including his challenge to authority, reversing the norms of culture and advocating an alternative form of wisdom, prompt us to examine more deeply the relationship that the Lord had with culture. Fortunately for us, in *Christ and Culture*, H. Richard Niebuhr has suggested a handful of ways providing varied "solutions" to this apparent dilemma. Initially he sees Christ *and* culture in conflict, historically and even today, with more "radical" ways of living the Christian life. Next, he views Christ *of* culture as a recognition of the fundamental agreement between Jesus and human society. His third basic "solution," Christ *above* culture, suggests that what Jesus says and does always trumps the dictates of culture. Niebuhr also sees two additional possibilities, *Christ and culture in paradox* and *Christ as the transformer of culture*. In the first, he suggests that the authority of Christ and culture are recognized as opposed ideas, but that this opposition is also accepted. Christians are subject to the tension accompanying these two authorities that apparently do not agree, yet both must be obeyed. Christians find themselves as subjects of two worlds that are not discontinuous, but largely opposed. Lastly, Christ as the *transformer of culture* sees the fallen nature of humanity and the need for Christ to transform society.

Our investigation has now one more important tool. Do we see Jesus in opposition to culture or more as the one who is integrated into and ultimately triumphs over society? Answering this question will indeed help us in our ultimate quest.

Discussion Questions

1. How does Christ's countercultural approach to life challenge you in living the Christian life today?
2. Is Jesus's message a hindrance to or an antidote for the progress of contemporary society?
3. Which of Niebuhr's "solutions" to the Christ and culture question is most attractive to you? Why?
4. As a contemporary Christian, what is your role in transforming culture more closely along the lines of Jesus's teachings?
5. What does it mean to you for a Christian to live *in* the world, but not *of* the world?

EPILOGUE

"Who do you say that I am?" the classic question Jesus poses to St. Peter, was relevant at that precise moment, for it gave the apostle the opportunity to make his famous confession of faith. It continues to have significance for Christians today. In our contemporary and increasingly secularized society, where answers to all dilemmas and difficulties are first sought in the realms of the material world, science and technology, the relevance of Jesus and his message is constantly debated. People of faith, barraged by the enticements of the world—power, wealth, and prestige—need to cling ever more closely to the message and mission of Jesus. Seeking a personal answer to Jesus's question to Peter can greatly facilitate our own ability to stand against the tidal wave of contemporary life seeking to drown out our voice. This book has been an attempt to give the readers many ideas whereby to know Jesus better, and allow them to discover a response to the Lord's challenging question.

We started our investigation by looking at what we know about Jesus from the basic sources of Scripture and history. The question, "Who is Jesus?" might seem like a query easily answered by people of faith. But the reality is that responses will vary, depending on how one experiences the presence of Christ in one's life. Thus, in order to set the basic foundation for our investigation, it was necessary to ask this seemingly mundane question. Once the foundation was set by providing possible answers to this basic query, then we could review what history has taught and the teachings of the Church tell us concerning

Jesus. While people today would routinely agree without even thinking about it that Jesus is the Son of God, the second person of the Blessed Trinity who is simultaneously both human and divine, we have learned that these basic dogmas of the faith took centuries to define. Such theological clarity became necessary as a result of heretical beliefs that began to circulate amongst the Christian faithful. Scripture, the basic tool that must be used to answer all questions concerning Christianity, while not providing dogmatic teachings about Jesus, does inform us of his actions and words and is, therefore, the basic source from which all ideas about Jesus must find their origins. We look at the concept of the Jesus of faith, the idea that all the actions of Christ are seen through the lens that he is a resurrected Savior and Son of God. This was juxtaposed to the Christ of history, a more contemporary post-Enlightenment perspective that sought to bring a more rigid and factual aspect to the life of Jesus. Where some might suggest that the Jesus of faith cannot be rigorously verified, there certainly is historical evidence that initiated this paradigm.

Completing our review of Scripture and history concerning Jesus, we next looked at the various roles that Christ manifested during the days of his public ministry. We saw in many ways that he was a "reverser of roles," turning many ideas and cultural norms of his day on their heads, transforming things 180 degrees in the opposite direction. When heroes such as scribes and Pharisees become villains and outcasts like the Samaritans, who now become insiders; when Jesus claimed that the last will be first and the first will be last; when he suggested that if you wish to be important be the servant of all, he was proclaiming a series of ideas that made virtually no sense to the people of his time. In many ways this countercultural approach to life has always been the lot of those who wish to follow in the footsteps of Jesus. Jesus also served in the role of teacher, not only for his chosen twelve apostles, but for the many disciples and others who heard the words of his mouth and observed the actions of his life. He showed men and women how to live and set proper priorities in life. Jesus also possessed a significant role as a moral decision maker. It can be debated whether the standards he met were impossible to uphold, utopian in nature, or if they were simply goals that we should try to emulate. The fact remains, however, that he set a pattern and gave guidelines, through his own life, to make proper moral decisions on our own. Lastly, Jesus was one who constantly spoke about the kingdom of God. Was his role to foreshadow the kingdom or to establish it during his lifetime? Again, the Scriptures are unclear, but they force us to ask, what was the Lord's role in this area? Overall, the various roles Jesus played provide significant input into how we might answer the question of this book's investigation.

After reviewing what history and Scripture say about Jesus, and examining the various roles he fulfilled during his earthly ministry, this inquiry closed by looking at the relationship of Jesus to culture and asking the question, "Why was Jesus executed?" Using Niebuhr's work, we found that Christ can be viewed in opposition to culture, in line with culture, or above culture. Each of these ideas has some historical precedence, but each is also problematic. Asking why Jesus was executed might seem an obvious question to many, yet as we have seen, the idea that he claimed to be a king, the Messiah, or even the Son of God, while certainly possible answers, are not exclusive. It can be argued that Jesus, from the perspective of the Jewish religious elite, was simply a rabble-rouser and lawbreaker, a generally problematic person who upset the contemporary status quo to such a degree that it was deemed necessary that he be eliminated. A review of the various roles Jesus held and how he manifested himself to others can easily support this latter conclusion.

Now at the conclusion of this study, where do we stand? Hopefully, the reader is much better informed on what Church and Scripture say about Jesus, and how his various roles have been understood by the Christian faithful over history, including and possibly most importantly, today. Having a better understanding of Jesus will in the end make Christians stronger, more faithful and dedicated, and better able to stand against the world, which today seeks to minimize the message of Christ, or suggest he is irrelevant for our contemporary world. Jesus's message, if lived faithfully, will always remain countercultural. While the world has advanced in many ways that have brought positive results for our society, it has too often been suggested that modernity does not need the message of Christ. Nothing, however, could be further from the truth; we need Jesus more today than in the recent past. Hopefully, armed with a greater understanding of Christ, his message, and his mission, we can all be better equipped to continue his basic ministry, building God's kingdom, brick by brick, day by day, to life eternal.

Discussion Questions

1. What role does faith in Christ play in your life? Is your faith in Jesus central, or is it one of many aspects of your day-to-day existence?
2. Pope Emeritus Benedict XVI once asked, "Where is the post-Easter faith supposed to come from if Jesus made no foundation for it before Easter?" How do you react to this question?
3. Which event in Jesus's life do you see as central to the Jesus of faith paradigm?

4. Why, in your opinion, did those who knew Jesus best not recognize him after the resurrection? Was Jesus trying to send a message to them, and by extension, all who would follow after them?

5. How does the Jesus of faith paradigm assist you in answering our question, "Who do you say that I am?"

NOTES

INTRODUCTION

1. The Second Vatican Council in its fundamental Dogmatic Constitution, *Dei Verbum*, The Constitution on Revelation, clearly teaches that there is one source of revelation that has three parts or components, Scripture, Sacred Tradition, and the Magisterium. See *Dei Verbum*, chap. 2, paras. 7–10.

CHAPTER 1

1. Marcus Borg, *Meeting Jesus Again for the First Time: The Historical Jesus and the Heart of Contemporary Faith* (San Francisco: Harper, 1994).

2. Vatican II, Dogmatic Constitution on Divine Revelation (*Dei Verbum*). When stating "in view of the situation of their churches," the Council fathers were suggesting that the gospel evangelists wrote to particular communities of faith, seeking to explain Jesus and his message to them in words and using images that were understandable to the audience. The intent of the evangelists, and by extension all of the New Testament writers, is not to write a precise history, but rather to communicate authoritatively and accurately the message of Jesus Christ, taking from his life and reports about him information that communicates an accurate message to those addressed.

3. Possibly the most illustrative passage in the Old Testament that describes the foretold Messiah, as was expected by the Jews, is Jeremiah 23:5–6: "The days are surely coming, says the LORD, when I will raise

up for David a righteous Branch, and he shall reign as king and deal wisely, and shall execute justice and righteousness in the land. In his days Judah will be saved and Israel will live in safety. And this is the name by which he will be called: 'The LORD is our righteousness.'" Thus, the Jews expected the Messiah to be a powerful ruler who would vanquish all of their enemies and restore the greatness of Israel. Clearly, Peter had a different perspective on the nature of the Messiah, possibly understanding Jesus more along the lines of the Suffering Servant passages of Isaiah; see Isaiah 52:13—53:12 as the classic example.

4. Joseph Ratzinger (Pope Benedict XVI), *Jesus of Nazareth: From the Baptism in the Jordan to the Transfiguration* (New York: Doubleday, 2007), 303.

CHAPTER 2

1. Henry Bettenson, ed. "The Definition of Chalcedon," in *Documents of the Christian Church*, 2nd ed. (London: Oxford University Press, 1967), 51–52.

CHAPTER 3

1. Roman Catholics hold seven additional books (Tobit, I and II Maccabees, Judith, Sirach, Wisdom, and Baruch) to be part of the Old Testament. These seven are collectively called the Apocrypha. Thus, Catholics hold that there are 46 books in the Old Testament.

2. Although there is no physical copy available to scholars today, biblical experts tell us that there is sufficient evidence to know that a Gospel, written in Aramaic, the spoken language of Jesus and the common people of his era in Israel, attributed to a man named Matthew, was available to the author of Mark's Gospel. Although the text is no longer extant (meaning not physically available), sufficient evidence does exist for its use in the composition of this Gospel.

3. The "Q source" (from the German quelle, meaning "source") is the name given to a common source utilized by both Luke and Matthew.

There are numerous stories in the Gospels that are contained only in Matthew and Luke. Examples include the parables of the lost sheep and lost coin, the parable of the great supper, the Our Father, instructions on love of one's enemies, the Beatitudes, and the cure of the centurion's servant. Biblical scholars conclude that since these (and other) accounts are only in these two Gospels, these documents share a common source that was not available to the other evangelists. Thus the name "Q source."

4. Acts 4:13 reads, "Now when they saw the boldness of Peter and John and realized that they were uneducated and ordinary men, they were amazed and recognized them as companions of Jesus." This verse indicates that John was probably not capable of writing the Gospel attributed to him.

5. The seven "I am" statements of John, for a Jew of Jesus's day, would have been bold proclamations; a knowledgeable person on the Scriptures would have directly associated these statements with Yahweh. In Exodus 3:14, Yahweh calls himself "I am." Jesus, was, in other words, claiming that he was God.

CHAPTER 5

1. Josh McDowell and Bill Wilson, *Evidence for the Historical Jesus: A Compelling Case for His Life and His Claims* (Eugene, Oregon: Harvest House Publishers, 1993), 32–51.

2. Apocrypha, meaning hidden, and pseudepigrapha, meaning false, are designations for texts that while written in the general time of the canonical Scriptures are not part of the Bible, as accepted by all Christians. Both Apocrypha and pseudepigrapha are useful, especially as seen in Sacred Tradition, which along with the Bible and the Magisterium comprise the one source of revelation.

3. Albert Schweitzer, *The Quest of the Historical Jesus: A Critical Study of Its Progress from Reimarus to Wrede* (New York: Macmillan, 1966), 398.

4. Redaction can be seen in simplistic terms by a simple illustration. Imagine a group of twenty people. The first person in this group

is asked to write a short essay using pen and paper. The task of the other nineteen is one by one to take the original essay and recopy it. In the process person number two cannot precisely read some words in the original text. Additionally, person number two decides to use a few synonyms rather than the precise words in the original. This person also adds a sentence or two for clarity. When person number three and all subsequent people have their opportunity to copy the original, it can easily be understood why what is produced by person number twenty will be in many ways quite different from the original. Biblical redaction seeks in a similar way to peel away the layers of the centuries and get back to the original text and meaning of the first evangelists and other authors.

CHAPTER 6

1. Michael H. Crosby, *The Prayer That Jesus Taught* (Maryknoll, NY: Orbis Books, 2002), 4.

2. St. Thomas Aquinas, *The Three Greatest Prayers: Commentaries on the Our Father, the Hail Mary and the Apostles' Creed*, trans. Laurence Shapcote (Westminster, MD: The Newman Press, 1956), 1.

3. Patricia Collins, "The Prayer of Our Lord: A Gospel View," *Spiritual Life* 31, 1 (1985): 21.

4. *Catechism of the Catholic Church* (Mahwah, NJ: Paulist Press, 1994), no. 2776.

5. The rationale behind the conclusion that Luke's version is most original is as follows. Scholars believe that it would be unthinkable for an evangelist to actually delete anything from Jesus's original words. It is conceivable, however, in their minds, that for reasons that might be helpful to the Jews, the audience of Matthew's Gospel, the evangelist added to the original text.

6. Joachim Jeremias, *Prayers of Jesus*, trans. Christoph Burchard (London: SCM Press, 1967), 76.

CHAPTER 11

1. This idea was based on Jesus's comment, "You have heard that it was said, 'An eye for an eye and a tooth for a tooth.' But I say to you, Do not resist an evildoer" (Matt 5:38–39).

2. Held in the year 49, the Council of Jerusalem (Acts 15) was transformative for the early Christian community. Using circumcision as his primary example, Paul argued that Gentiles did not have to follow all of the precepts of the Mosaic Law in order to become Christians. While more conservative Jewish-Christians, such as the Judaizers, believed that adherence to the law was an absolute necessity, Paul won the argument when discussing the same with James, the leader of the Jerusalem Church, and others present at the meeting. This decision allowed Christianity to become its own world religion rather than remaining a sect of Judaism.

SELECT BIBLIOGRAPHY FOR ADDITIONAL READING

JESUS CHRIST

Barrett, Charles K. *Jesus and the Gospel Tradition*. Philadelphia: Fortress Press, 1968.

Barter Moulaison, Jane. *Thinking Christ: Christology and Contemporary Critics*. Minneapolis, MN: Fortress Press, 2012.

Beilby, James K., and Paul Rhodes Eddy. *The Historical Jesus: Five Views*. Downers Grove, IL: InterVarsity Press, 2009.

Boff, Leonardo. *Jesus Christ Liberator: A Critical Christology for Our Times*. Translated by Patrick Hughes. Maryknoll, NY: Orbis Books, 1978.

Bonagura, David G. "Joseph Ratzinger/Benedict XVI's Christology of Jesus' Prayer and Two Contemporary Theological Questions," *Nova et Vetera* 12, no. 1 (2014): 287–306.

Borg, Marcus J. *Jesus: The Life, Teachings, and Relevance of a Religious Revolutionary.* San Francisco: HarperCollins, 2006.

———. *Meeting Jesus Again for the First Time: The Historical Jesus and the Heart of the Contemporary Life*. San Francisco: HarperCollins, 1994.

Borg, Marcus J., and N.T. Wright. *The Meaning of Jesus: Two Visions.* San Francisco: HarperCollins, 2000.

Boucher, Madeleine. *The Parables*. Wilmington, DE: Michael Glazier, 1983.

Braun, Herbert. *Jesus of Nazareth: The Man and His Time*. Translated by Everett Kalin. Philadelphia: Fortress Press, 1979.

Burroughs, Jonathan. "Jesus and the Law in the Gospel of Matthew," *Doctrine and Life* 64, no. 10 (2014): 45–58.

Capps, Donald. *Jesus: A Psychological Biography*. St. Louis: Chalice Press, 2000.

Crossan, John Dominic. *The Historical Jesus: The Life of a Mediterranean Jewish Peasant*. San Francisco: HarperCollins, 1991.

———. *Jesus: A Revolutionary Biography*. San Francisco: HarperCollins, 1989.

———. *The Power of Parable: How Fiction by Jesus Became Fiction about Jesus*. New York: HarperOne, 2012.

Daniel-Rops, Henri. *Jesus and His Times*. New York: Dutton, 1956.

Drury, John. *The Parables in the Gospels: History and Allegory*. New York: Crossroad, 1985.

Dunn, James. *Did the First Christians Worship Jesus?: The New Testament Evidence*. Louisville, KY: Westminster John Knox Press, 2010.

———. *Jesus Remembered*. Grand Rapids, MI: Wm. B. Eerdmans, 2003.

Dupuis, Jacques. *Who Do You Say That I Am?: Introduction to Christology*. Maryknoll, NY: Orbis Books, 1994.

Eckhardt, A. Roy. *Reclaiming the Jesus of History Christology Today*. Minneapolis, MN: Fortress Press, 1992.

Endo, Shusaku. *A Life of Jesus*. Translated by Richard A. Schuchert. New York: Paulist Press, 1973.

Ford, David F., and Mike Higton, eds. *Jesus*. New York: Oxford University Press, 2002.

Fortna, Robert T., and Tom Thatcher, eds. *Jesus in Johannine Tradition*. Louisville, KY: Westminster John Knox Press, 2001.

Gaine, Simon. "The Veracity of Prophecy and Christ's Knowledge." *New Blackfriars* 98, no. 1073 (2017): 44–62.

Gowler, David B. *What Are They Saying About the Historical Jesus?* New York: Paulist Press, 2007.

———. *What Are They Saying About the Parables?* New York: Paulist Press, 2000.

Herzog, II, William R. *Prophet and Teacher: An Introduction to the Historical Jesus*. Louisville, KY: Westminster John Knox Press, 2005.

Hoffman, Dominic M., and Basil Cole. "The Incarnation (Part II): The Mystery of How Jesus is God and Man at the Same Time." *The Priest* 70, no. 4 (2014): 20.

Hoppe, Leslie J. "Jesus Family Tomb?" *The Bible Today* 52, no. 5 (2014): 293–300.

Hurtado, Larry W. *Lord Jesus Christ: Devotion to Jesus in Earliest Christianity* (Grand Rapids, MI: Wm. B. Eerdmans, 2003.

Imbelli, Robert P. "The Christocentric Mystagogy of Joseph Ratzinger." *Communio* 42, no. 1 (2015): 119–43.

Jeremias, Joachim. *The Parables of Jesus*. New York: Scribner, 1963.

Johnson, Luke T. *Prophetic Jesus, Prophetic Church: The Challenge of Luke-Acts to Contemporary Christians*. Grand Rapids, MI: Wm. B. Eerdmans, 2011.

———. *The Real Jesus: The Misguided Quest for the Historical Jesus and the Truth of the Traditional Gospel.* San Francisco: HarperCollins, 1996.

Johnson, Paul. *Jesus: A Biography from a Believer*. New York: Penguin Books, 2011.

Kaylor, R. David. *Jesus the Prophet: His Vision of the Kingdom on Earth*. Louisville, KY: Westminster John Knox Press, 1994.

Keck, Leander E. *Who Is Jesus?: History in Perfect Tense*. Columbia, SC: University of South Carolina Press, 2000.

King, Nicholas. "The Historical Reliability of John's Gospel," *ET Studies* 6, no. 1 (2015): 31–43.

Klausner, Joseph. *Jesus of Nazareth: His Life, Times, and Teaching*. Translated by Herbert Danby. New York: Menorah Publishing Company, 1979.

Knitter, Paul. *Jesus and the Other Names: Christian Mission and Global Responsibility*. Maryknoll, NY: Orbis Books, 1996.

Levine, Amy-Jill. *Short Stories by Jesus: The Enigmatic Parables of a Controversial Rabbi*. San Francisco: HarperOne, 2014.

Levine, Amy-Jill, Dale C. Allison Jr., and John Dominic Crossan, eds. *The Historical Jesus in Context.* Princeton, NJ: Princeton University Press, 2006.

"Life in Christ: Morals, Communion and the Church: An Agreed Statement by ARCIC-II." *One in Christ* 30, no. 4 (1994): 355–87.

McDowell, Josh, and Bill Wilson. *Evidence for the Historical Jesus: A Compelling Case for His Life and Claims.* Eugene, OR: Harvest House Publishers, 1988.

Meier, John P. *A Marginal Jew: Rethinking the Historical Jesus.* Vol. 1. New York: Doubleday: 1991.

———. *A Marginal Jew: Rethinking the Historical Jesus: Companions and Competitors*. Vol. 3. New York: Doubleday, 2001.

———. *A Marginal Jew: Rethinking the Historical Jesus: Mentors, Message and Miracles*. Vol. 2. New York: Doubleday, 1994.

Michaels, J. Ramsey. *Servant and Son: Jesus in Parable and Gospel.* Atlanta: John Knox Press, 1981.

Moltmann, Jurgen. *Jesus Christ for Today's World.* Translated by Margaret Kohl. Minneapolis, MN: Fortress Press, 1994.

Neibuhr, H. Richard. *Christ and Culture*. New York: Harper Torch Books, 1951.

O'Collins, Gerald. *Easter Faith: Believing in the Risen Jesus*. Mahwah, NJ: Paulist Press, 2003.

———. *Jesus: A Portrait*. Maryknoll, NY: Orbis Books, 2008.

———. "The Presence of Christ." *The Pastoral Review* 10, no. 1 (2014): 10–13.

O'Connell, Seamus. "The Family of Jesus in the Gospels." *The Bible Today* 53, no. 1 (2015): 19–25.

O'Malley, William J. "The Moral Practice of Jesus." *America* 170 (April 23, 1994): 8–10.

Powell, Mark Allan. *Jesus as a Figure in History: How Modern Historians View the Man from Galilee*. Louisville, KY: Westminster John Knox Press, 2013.

Ratzinger, Joseph (Pope Benedict XVI). *Jesus of Nazareth*. New York: Doubleday, 2007.

Reid, Barbara E. "Jesus: Parabolic Preacher." *The Bible Today* 52, no. 4 (2014): 207–11.

Robinson, James M. *Jesus: According to the Earliest Witness.* Minneapolis, MN: Fortress Press, 2007.

Sanders, E.P. *The Historical Figure of Jesus*. London: Allen Lane Penguin Books, 1993.

Schillebeeckx, Edward. *Jesus: An Experiment in Christology*. New York: Crossroads, 1981.

Schillebeeckx, Edward and Bas Van Iersel, eds. *Jesus Christ and Human Freedom*. New York: Herder and Herder, 1974.

Schottroff, Luise. *The Parables of Jesus*. Minneapolis, MN: Fortress Press, 2006.

Sloyan, Gerald S. *The Jesus Tradition: Images of Jesus in the West*. Mystic, CT: Twenty-Third Publications, 1986.

———. *Why Jesus Died*. Minneapolis, MN: Fortress Press, 2004.

Snodgrass, Klyne. *Stories with Intent: A Comprehensive Guide to the Parables of Jesus*. Grand Rapids, MI: Wm. B. Eerdmans, 2008.

Stein, Robert H. *The Method and Message of Jesus' Teaching*. Louisville, KY: Westminster John Knox Press, 1994.

Theissen, Gerd. *The Shadow of the Galilean: The Quest of the Historical Jesus in Narrative Form*. Philadelphia: Fortress Press, 1987.

Trocme, Andre. *Jesus and the Nonviolent Revolution*. Translated by Michael H. Shank and Marlin E. Miller. Scottdale, PA: Herald Press, 1973.

Vermes, Geza. *Jesus and the World of Judaism*. Philadelphia: Fortress Press, 1984.

———. *The Religion of Jesus the Jew*. Philadelphia: Fortress Press, 1994.

Weiss, Johannes. *Jesus' Proclamation of the Kingdom of God*. Translated by Richard Hyde Heirs and David Larrimore. Philadelphia: Fortress Press, 1971.

Welch, Lawrence J. "Christ, the Moral Law, and the Teaching Authority of the Magisterium." *Irish Theological Quarterly* 64, no. 1 (September 1999):16–28.

Westermann, Claus. *The Parables of Jesus in Light of the Old Testament*. Translated by Friedermann W. Golka and Alastair Logan. Edinburgh, Scotland: T & T Clark, 1990.

Wilkins, Jeremy. "Who Is Jesus of Nazareth?: Insights from Lonergan's Christology." *The Lonergan Review* 6, no. 1 (2015): 51–76.

Wills, Gary. *What Jesus Meant*. New York: Viking Press, 2006.

Wright, N.T. *The Challenge of Jesus: Rediscovering Where Jesus Was and Is*. Downers Grove, IL: InterVarsity Press, 1999.

———. *The Original Jesus: The Life and Vision of a Revolutionary*. Grand Rapids, MI: Wm. B. Eerdmans, 1996.

———. *Who Was Jesus?* Grand Rapids, MI: Wm. B. Eerdmans, 1993.

Yoder Neufeld, Thomas R. *Recovering Jesus: The Witness of the New Testament*. Grand Rapids, MI: Brazos Press, 2007.

Younge, Pat. "The Name of Jesus: A Reflection, in the Year of the Holy Name." *Religious Life Review* 53, no. 286 (2014): 189–92.

PARABLE AND SCRIPTURE

Boucher, Madeleine I. *The Mysterious Parable: A Literary Study*. Washington, DC: The Catholic Biblical Association of America, 1977.

Collins, Raymond F. "Parables for Priests: The Lost Sheep." *Emmanuel* 109, no. 1 (January/February 2003): 11–21.

Donahue, John. *The Gospel in Parable*. Philadelphia: Fortress Press, 1988.

Doohan, Leonard. "Parables and Miracles." *Modern Liturgy* 20 (May 1993): 34–35.

Gribble, Richard. *The Parables of Jesus: Applications for Contemporary Life, Cycle A*. Lima, OH: CSS Publishing, 1998.

———. *The Parables of Jesus: Applications for Contemporary Life, Cycle B*. Lima, OH: CSS Publishing, 1999.

———. *The Parables of Jesus: Applications for Contemporary Life, Cycle C*. Lima, OH: CSS Publishing, 2000.

Harrington, Wilfrid J. *A Key to the Parables*. Glen Rock, NJ: Paulist Press, 1964.

Hedrick, Charles W. *Many Things in Parables: Jesus and His Modern Critics*. Louisville, KY: Westminster John Knox Press, 2004.

Hensell, Eugene. "Encountering the Parables of Jesus." *Review for Religious* 64, no. 3 (2005): 316–20.

Hughes, Gerard W. "Parables of the Spirit." *Tablet* (London) 248 (October 8, 1994): 1262–63.

Karban, Roger V. "Exploring the Parables of Jesus." *Liguorian* 92, no. 7 (September 2004): 28–31.

Kilgallen, John J. "Parables in the Gospel of Luke." *Chicago Studies* 38 (Fall/Winter 1999): 273–82.

Longenecker, Richard N., ed. *The Challenge of Jesus' Parables*. Grand Rapids, MI: Wm. B. Eerdmans, 2000.

MacArthur, John F. *The Gospel According to Jesus: What Does Jesus Mean When He Says "Follow Me?"* Grand Rapids, MI: Zondervan, 1994.

Marshall, Gordian. "Parables: Jewish and Christian." *Priests & People* 14, no. 7 (July 2000): 270–74.

Mitchell, Stephen. *The Gospel According to Jesus: A New Translation and Guide to His Essential Teachings for Believers and Unbelievers*. New York: HarperCollins, 1991.

Pagels, Elaine. *The Gnostic Gospels*. New York: Vintage Books, 1981.

Parks, Ted. "Parables of Jarring Reality." *National Catholic Reporter* 38, no. 9 (December 28, 2001): 10–11.

Perkins, Pheme. *Hearing the Parables of Jesus*. New York: Paulist Press, 1981.

Phillips, Jim. "Kingdom Parables." *Religion Teachers' Journal* 36, no. 1 (February 2002): 10–11.

Reid, Barbara E. "Lukan Parables in the Lectionary." *Bible Today* 38 (November/December 2000): 343–48.

Smith, Charles William. *The Jesus of the Parables*. Philadelphia: Fortress Press, 1975.

Stein, Robert H. *An Introduction to the Parables of Jesus*. Philadelphia: Westminster Press, 1981.

Thomas, Clemens, and Michael Wyschogrod, eds. *Parable and Story in Judaism and Christianity*. New York: Paulist Press, 1989.